# Home
## Sweet Sewn

# Home
## Sweet Sewn

Alice Butcher & Ginny Farquhar

D&C
David and Charles
www.rucraft.co.uk

A DAVID & CHARLES BOOK
Copyright © David & Charles Limited 2009

David & Charles is an F+W Media Inc. company
4700 East Galbraith Road
Cincinnati, OH 45236

First published in the UK in 2009

Text and designs copyright © Alice Butcher and Ginny Farquhar 2009

Alice Butcher and Ginny Farquhar have asserted their right to be identified as authors of this work in accordance with the Copyright, Designs and Patents Act, 1988.

A catalogue record for this book is available from the British Library.

ISBN-13: 978-0-7153-3286-3 paperback
ISBN-10: 0-7153-3286-4 paperback

Printed in China by R R Donnelley
for David & Charles
Brunel House     Newton Abbot     Devon

Commissioning Editor: Jennifer Fox-Proverbs
Editor: Bethany Dymond
Assistant Editor: Kate Nicholson
Project Editor: Cathy Joseph
Art Editors: Prudence Rogers and Sarah Clark
Designer: Mia Farrant
Production Controller: Bev Richardson and Alison Smith
Photographer: Sian Irvine

Visit our website at www.davidandcharles.co.uk

David & Charles books are available from all good bookshops; alternatively you can contact our Orderline on 0870 9908222 or write to us at FREEPOST EX2 110, D&C Direct, Newton Abbot, TQ12 4ZZ (no stamp required UK only); US customers call 800-289-0963 and Canadian customers call 800-840-5220.

# Contents

# introduction

Home is where the heart is. For some it is the sanctuary that we return to after a grueling day at work, for others the place where we spend our days. All of us want our house to be a home – somewhere to relax, spend time with family or entertain. Likewise, we want our homes to express a part of ourselves, whether it's a country cottage with a kitchen dresser filled with knick-knacks and colourful crockery or a minimalist, chic apartment space with a few considered objects for decoration. These are the things that make our homes individual and special to us.

Ever passionate about collecting, thrifting and recycling fabrics, giving them a twist and creating something new, we have devised a collection of 23 projects for the home that are either functional or frivolous but always fun! All the projects within this book grew out of seasonal inspirations and the cycle of the year. We hope to give you an insight into our creative process, showing you how our ideas evolve from fabric swatches, sketches, photos and even poems to become a working design and finished piece.

You may wish to recreate the projects as we have shown them in the book, but we are sure that many of you will use the patterns and images as a starting point and bring your ideas and designs to them. Included within the book are many different techniques including photo-montage, appliqué, embroidery, crazy patchwork, stenciling and rag rugging, any of which may start your own crafting obsession! Most projects include a design inspiration offering you alternative design ideas, but why not put your own creative stamp upon these projects taking inspiration from the things you love and that mean something to you?

Our year commences with planning, spring cleaning and getting the house in order. Use your favourite photos to create a useful monthly wall planner with handy pockets or recycle old pinstripe shirts to make an alternative version for the office. Our sweet appliqué song thrush apron will encourage you to pick up the duster and clean your nest! Preserve the memory of your home in stitch using hand appliqué, patchwork and embroidery. For a bold design statement, dig out your retro pillowcases and sheets and transform them into a fresh, modern duvet, pillowcase and linen bag.

Warmer days bring flowers and strawberries with the vintage linen inspired tea set and funky stencilled picnic blanket projects and if those rainy days show up, bring the garden inside with our fun quilted floor game featuring roses and garden creatures.

Inspired by the warm earthy tones of fall and the need to make our homes cosy, we move on to create a beautiful throw designed with collected leaves, a rich rag rug made from recycled T-shirts and a timeless, classic, shaker-style tree of life cushion with crisp apple appliqués.

As the year draws to an end and the weather becomes colder, thoughts turn to the festive season. The classic holly leaf has been interpreted in fabric to make a contemporary wreath embellished with ceramic beads and buttons. A soft lilac floral version finished with crystal beads and mother-of-pearl buttons could be used throughout the year. Make a beautiful heirloom angel doll using crazy patchwork in vintage linens and decorate the Christmas tree with some gorgeous hanging stars. For a lasting reminder, construct a memory book incorporating motifs of the year and filled with family mementos, stories and keepsakes.

We hope you will enjoy reading this book and creating the projects as much as we have enjoyed putting them together. We also hope that our book will inspire you to create some home sweet sewn projects for your home.

# getting organized

Many of us enjoy the creativity and ease of taking photographs with our digital cameras. Sadly, most of these photos remain in files on the computer and are too easily forgotten. To kick start a New Year and become a little more efficient, this fabulous monthly wall planner is a great way of displaying some of your much loved pictures whilst organizing yourself and the family.

Choose your favourite photos or images to print on to fabric and make a montage of memories. With 31 numbered pockets and removable month banners, jot down notes or reminders and insert into the pockets and make some decorative pins to attach for those special occasions, such as a family birthday or anniversary.

'Organizing is what you do before you do something, so that when you do it, it's not all mixed up.'
A.A. MILNE

## You will need

- 90 x 60cm (35¼ x 23½in) linen for the planner front
- 1m x 140cm (39¼ x 55in) linen for the pockets and the months
- 1m x 140cm (39¼ x 55in) calico for the pocket linings and month banners
- 20 x 10cm (8 x 4in) each of five different patterned fabric scraps for the numbers
- 90 x 60cm (35¼ x 23½in) canvas for interlining
- 96 x 66cm (37¾ x 26in) patterned cotton for backing
- 25 x 90cm (9¾ x 35¼in) fusible interfacing for monthly banners
- Two small buttons to attach month banners
- Scraps of fabric and coloured felt for pins
- Approx. 1m x 140cms (39¼ x 55in) calico or specially prepared fabric for printing
- Ink-jet printer with colour printer ink
- Photocopier with ink-jet printer (not laser printer)
- A selection of photos, postcards or pressed flowers
- 60cm (23½in) double-sided fusible webbing (Bondaweb)
- Approx. 10 Sheets of freezer paper
- 20cm (8in) thin twine
- Five large eyelets
- Denim needle
- Coloured embroidery threads

You'll find the templates for this project on pages 110–111

## Prepare

*One* First cut out your linen top fabric and canvas interlining to the exact measurements given in the 'You will need' list. Mount the interlining on to the reverse of the linen with pins and tack together around the s/a. Transfer through all your markings and placement lines (refer to the pattern on pages 110–111). Stitch a tacking line on to these markings so that you can see them from the right side.

*Two* Choose your images. For our planner we have used 14 small, bordered images taken from photographs stored on the computer. In addition, we printed off a further five images such as the pumpkin, apple and robin that would work well as cut out shapes. The cut out flower shapes are taken from pressed flowers that were just photocopied.

*Three* Next, play around with your chosen images and work out their sizing and positioning. If you are using images from your computer, re-size and save them in your photo-editing program. To create the effect we have, aim for good quality images sized to between 5 x 5cm (2 x 2in) and 14 x 10cm (5½ x 4in). All photocopiers have a sizing option to enable you to scale images up and down by a percentage. Remember to make a note of the percentage that you have reduced (or enlarged) them to.

*Four* Take time planning your photo-montage. Print out or photocopy all of your chosen images on to paper and lay these on the top half of the linen. Move around until you are happy with the placing. Remember to leave a space of about 24 x 6cm (9½ x 2⅜in) for the monthly banner and buttons **(a)**.

*a*

There are so many different options for decorating your planner, you can really let loose your imagination, have fun and create a montage that holds meaning for you.

## Print to fabric

*One* Cut out as many calico rectangles as you need for printing your images. Make sure that they are 3cm (1⅛in) smaller than your freezer paper. To protect your printer rollers, ensure that all edges are straight and free from loose threads. Place the shiny side of the freezer paper face down on to the calico and press. The calico will adhere temporarily to the freezer paper, allowing it to be fed through a printer.

*Two* First, have a trial print to ensure that your printer rollers are clean and that the print quality is good. Put the freezer paper backed calico into the printer and select your first image. When you are ready to print, select the paper option for photo printing. If you are photocopying, feed the freezer paper backed calico through in the same way.

*Three* Once you are happy with the print quality and positioning, print out or photocopy all of your images, then leave to dry. Peel off the freezer paper and place the printed calico face down on to a blank piece of paper. Gently iron on the reverse with a warm iron to remove any excess ink residue. Iron some Bondaweb on to the reverse of each image and cut out with a small 3mm (⅛in) border. For fun shapes such as the bird or pumpkin, cut out closely around the shape.

*Four* To arrange, remove the Bondaweb backings and carefully take up your paper mock-ups piece by piece and replace with the fabric images. Fuse the montage under a pressing cloth. Stitch on all shapes with a topstitch. Difficult curved shapes such as the flowers can be stitched on with freehand machine embroidery.

*Five* Choose a font style and size to approx. 48. Type out the months, January to December, making sure that you have at least a 1.5cm (⅝in) space around each word. Choose a colour, save and print out on to freezer paper backed calico. Put this to one side until later.

### Collect and copy
If you don't have a computer or digital camera, you can create a beautiful montage using conventional photographs with an ink-jet photocopier. You could combine these with images of wine labels, stamps, postcards, a child's sketch or note.

## Make the pocket strips

*One* Cut out the linen pocket strips and calico linings. Place one linen and one calico strip with r/s together and stitch both long sides. Turn through and press. Transfer the inverted pleat markings. Repeat with all pocket strips **(b)**. Note that the fifth strip is a different length. This is the bottom strip with the numbers 29, 30 and 31 and then two large pockets for reminder pins and notepaper.

*Two* Print out numbers 1–31 in a suitable font and size, then draw in reverse on to the smooth side of the Bondaweb. We have chosen five different fabrics for each row of seven. Fuse on to your chosen fabrics, cut out and position at the centre of each pocket front. Hold in place with a machine stitch through the centre of each number. Add an image on to each of the two large pockets on the bottom row as per Print to fabric instructions (page 11).

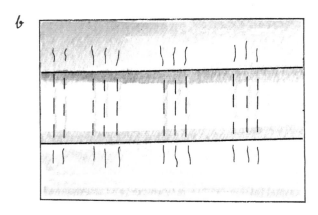

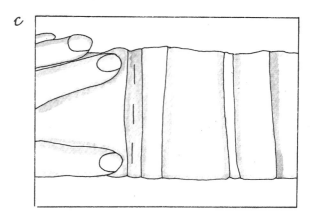

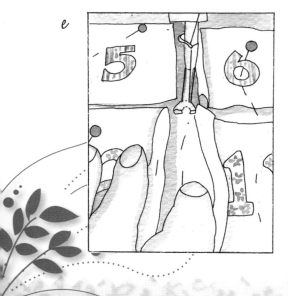

*Three* Take a pocket strip and create the inverted pleats for your seven pockets by pressing each marked foldline towards the pleat centre, referring to the pattern on page 111 **(c)**.

*Four* Repeat with all the pocket strips. Pop some pins in to hold in place and position the bottom edge of the pocket strips on to the placement lines on the planner in number order. Place a pin through the centre of each pocket front to hold in place and tack the centre of each pleat into position through all layers **(d)**.

*Five* Holding the pocket pleats open, machine stitch the centres into place starting at the top row and working each vertical column at a time **(e)**. Double back at the start and finish of each pocket to secure well. Trim ends, and repeat with each column. Roll the planner to reduce bulk and aid stitching.

**Six** Remove pins and press the pocket pleats closed. Tack the pockets into place along the placement lines and, with a denim needle, machine stitch into position **(f)**. Trim ends, remove tacking stitches and give a final press.

## Month banners and pins

**One** Fuse a piece of interfacing to a calico rectangle 24 x 12cm (9½ x 4¾in). Press in the short edges 1cm (⅜in). Fold in half along the long edge, r/s together and stitch leaving the short ends open. Turn through and press. Cut two pieces of twine 10cm (4in) long and knot each one to form loops. Insert the loops into each end, making sure that the loop is the perfect size to fit snugly over your button. Pin and topstitch closed. Repeat with 11 more calico rectangles.

**Two** Cut 12 linen rectangles 24 x 6cm (9½ x 23/8in). Topstitch 1cm (⅜in) from the edge and fray back by 5mm (³⁄₁₆in). Cut out the 12 printed month names with a 5mm (³⁄₁₆in) border and centre on to each piece of linen. Topstitch to attach. Pin the linen on to the calico rectangle and hand sew with a running stitch. Using Stitch and Tear (see page 106), transfer each relevant month motif on to the linen, about 2cm (¾in) either side or the wording, and embroider in your chosen colours.

**Three** To make a pin, draw out a simple design and trace on to Bondaweb. Fuse to your chosen scrap of fabric, cut out and press on to the coloured felt. Stitch to neaten with a small zigzag. Attach a small safety pin to the reverse.

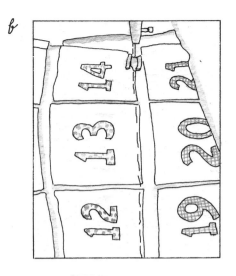

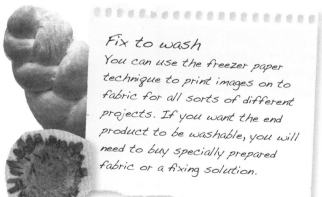

*Fix to wash*
You can use the freezer paper technique to print images on to fabric for all sorts of different projects. If you want the end product to be washable, you will need to buy specially prepared fabric or a fixing solution.

## Finish

**One** Cut out the backing cloth. This should be 3cm (1⅛in) larger than the planner all round. Lay the planner on top of the backing cloth with w/s together and with 3cm (1⅛in) of the backing showing at each edge. Pin together and tack around the outside edge just inside the s/a. Press over the backing 3cm (1⅛in) towards the front. Press under 1.5cm (⅝in) and pin. Fold the corners at right angles and topstitch into position.

**Two** Complete the wall planner by making five eyelets along the top edge (refer to the pattern for positioning). Sew on two buttons to hold the month banners. Hang the planner from picture hooks.

# pin-striped planner

Our variation shows the planner in formal suiting and pinstripe shirting with a simple patchwork theme and would be ideal for an office or workplace.

## You will need

- 90 x 60cm (35¼ x 23½in) suiting for the planner front
- 90 x 60cm (35¼ x 23½in) canvas for planner interlining
- 96 x 66cm (37¾ x 26in) ticking for backing
- Old pinstripe and formal work shirts for the pockets, numbers and patchwork
- 1m (39¼in) calico for pocket lining and month banners
- 40 x 140cm (15¾ x 55in) linen for mounting patchwork and month banners
- 25 x 90cm (9¾ x 35¼in) fusible interfacing for monthly banners
- 40 x 45cm (15¾ x 17¾in) suiting for the monthly banners
- Four sheets of freezer paper for printing and templates
- Two small buttons
- 20cm (8in) twine
- Grey embroidery thread
- Five large eyelets
- Scraps of fabric and coloured felt for pins

You'll find the templates for this project on pages 111–113

*One* Prepare the base cloths by following step one (page 10) of the family wall planner instructions.

*Two* Create the star patchwork by drawing out your templates on to freezer paper. Fuse shiny side down to the w/s of your chosen fabrics. Leaving a 7mm (⁹⁄₃₂in) s/a around each shape, cut out. Press over edges to w/s and tack in place. Construct the star by referring to the design layout. Place two diamond patches r/s together and with a small stitch, over sew together along one straight edge. Continue adding the diamonds to make up the star. Then, in the same way, add the triangles, the squares and finally add the border.

*Three* Cut out a piece of linen 35 x 40cm (13¾ x 15¾in). Stitch 5mm (³⁄₁₆in) just inside each edge and fray back to 2mm (¹⁄₁₀in). Stitch to the top part of the planner. Place the completed star patchwork over the linen and slipstitch all around.

*Four* Cut out 35 rectangles in a variety of different pinstripe, plain and check shirt fabrics, referring to the pocket patterns on pages 112–113. Pin together in strips of seven and sew, following the templates to place the larger left and right hand pockets. Complete the pockets following steps one to six for pocket strips as in the photo-montage planner (pages 12–13).

*Five* To finish, make up the calico monthly banners following the instructions for the photo-montage planner (page 13). Print the months using the freezer paper technique (page 11) on to some linen and apply to a strip of the suiting. Assemble the planner as before, back with ticking and complete with eyelets.

### Perfect pins

Pins can be made using scraps of fabric and felt and attached as reminders. A clock face pin for an appointment, a monetary symbol for pay day or an aeroplane to remember business trips would all work well.

# feathering the nest

As the seasons change and the birds begin to build their nests, we too turn our attention to the yearly spring-cleaning ritual and begin to get our own 'nests' in order. The springtime birds have given us the inspiration to create this pretty yet utilitarian work apron, perfect for carrying dusters, polish and cloths.

The front pockets are appliquéd with a simple song thrush happily sitting on a branch opposite her nest, which holds her clutch of speckled eggs. The body of the apron is made up using an eco cotton/hemp mix, which washes well with limited creasing and is a great base for appliqué work. The bias binding is created from duck egg blue linen, recycled from an old smock top.

'Here in the fork the brown nest is seated;
four little blue eggs the mother keeps heated.'
ROBERT LOUIS STEVENSON

## You will need

- 100 x 115cm (39½ x 45in) natural coloured cotton/hemp or cotton canvas for the apron and straps
- 115 x 2cm (45 x ¾in) bias binding in duck egg blue
- 50 x 10cm (20 x 4in) light brown wool fabric for the branch and nest texture
- Cut two straps 110 x 6cm (39¼ x 2⅜in) from natural coloured cotton/hemp or cotton canvas
- Cut one loop 11 x 5cm (4¼ x 2in) in duck egg blue lightweight cotton or linen
- Fabric scraps in browns, duck egg blue and cream cotton for the bird, nest and eggs
- Dark brown wool fabric scraps for nest texture
- Ten leaves in green wool fabric scraps
- Twine and feathers for nest decoration
- Double-sided fusible webbing (Bondaweb)
- Multi-purpose sewing threads
- Denim needle

You'll find the pattern for this project on page 113

## Prepare

*One* Scale up the apron pattern pieces including markings and cut out all the pieces.

*Two* To make up the apron pocket, press the front top edge over towards the r/s by 1cm (⅜in). Press over on the foldline towards the r/s and pin in place. Secure with topstitching, using a contrast thread.

## Add the appliqué

*One* Using the template on page 113, draw up the bird, nest, eggs and branch in reverse on to Bondaweb. Fuse the design on to your chosen fabrics, cut out and position on to the front apron pocket. Fuse the bird, nest, eggs and branch design into place. Machine appliqué (see page 107) around the nest pieces, then machine straight stitch around the branches, bird, tail detail and eggs **(a)**.

*Two* To create the texture on the nest, fuse two squares of Bondaweb measuring 6 x 6cm (2⅜ x 2⅜in) on to the dark and light brown wool fabric scraps. Cut thin strips of each colour in various sizes – on average 2.5mm x 3cm (⅛in x 1⅛in). Lay these fabric strips over your nest edge and when you are satisfied with their placement, fuse into position. Machine straight stitch along the centre of each strip to secure them, doubling back at each end. Trim or leave the thread ends as desired **(b)**. Cut up some tiny strips of twine, place in position and attach by hand using catch stitch.

*a*

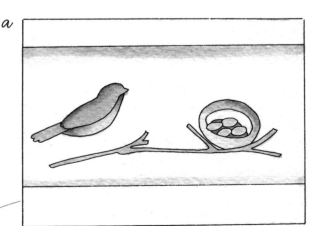

*b*

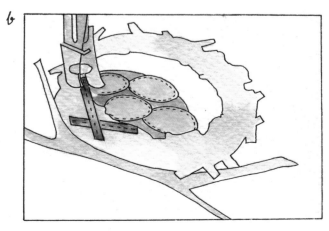

*Three* Using a dark grey or brown embroidery thread, add detail to the bird's underside with small v-shaped stitches. Sew speckled details on to the eggs using a stab stitch, then stem stitch the bird's legs, claws and eye and the detail on the wings and tail.

*Four* Draw ten small leaf shapes on to Bondaweb and fuse on to the scrap of green wool. Cut out the leaves, position them along the branch and fuse into place. Stitch in leaf detail to secure and hand stitch feathers into the nest and twine in the bird's beak.

*Line their nest*
Help the birds by leaving out nesting material. Anything natural that won't stay wet will do, for example feathers from an old pillow, moss from raking the lawn or tiny scraps of wool.

Here's your chance to try 'nesting' for yourself. You build the nest just like a bird would, layering up different materials until you are happy with the effect.

## Make up the apron

*One* To create the back of the apron piece, begin by turning in the top edge by 1cm (⅜in) towards w/s, then a further 1cm (⅜in). Press well and topstitch in place to secure. With the r/s facing up, place the apron pocket over the apron back and match up the bottom curved edge. From the front, pin on the bias binding around the curve. Stitch and clip the curves, trimming back to 1cm (⅜in) if necessary **(c)**.

*Two* Trim back the corners at each end to reduce bulk. Press the bias towards the back. Pin and stitch into position using machine topstitch or hand slipstitch. Press well. Over sew the two top ends by hand to neaten.

*Three* To create the pockets, start at the top and stitch 2.5mm (⅛in) away from the centre front down one side, across at the bottom, then up the other side, then another 2.5mm (⅛in) away from the centre front. Stitch across at the top to join the beginning of the stitch line.

*Four* Take one strap, turn in and press 1cm (⅜in) on one short edge. Press in half along the length with w/s together and turn in both long raw edges by 1cm (⅜in). Press, pin and machine topstitch the strap, using the denim needle to neaten. Repeat for the other strap **(d)**.

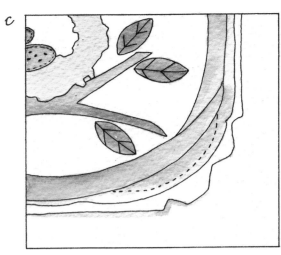

c

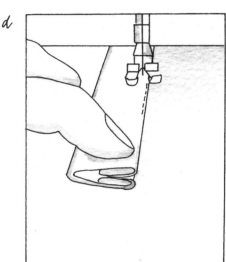

d

### Design Inspiration
This would also make a great gardening apron. On one pocket you could appliqué a little plant pot with a seedling sprouting out of the top and on the other packs of seeds and garden twine.

### Chores
- Dust cobwebs
- Wipe down paintwork
- Clean windows
- Turn mattresses
- Wash chair covers
- Take down curtains to be laundered

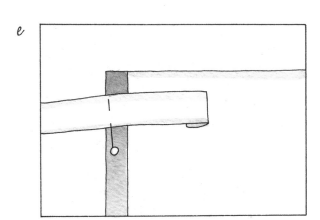

*e*

**Five** Press in 2cm (¾in) on the remaining raw edge of the strap. Measure along 7cm (2¾in) and mark with a pin. Position at the strap point on the w/s of the apron back, pin and stitch. Repeat with the second strap **(e)**.

**Six** To complete the apron, make a loop by taking the loop piece and stitching a channel with r/s together. Turn through and press. Press over each raw edge and pin to the apron, allowing a little give to enable a duster to be pulled through. Stitch into position with a little rectangle and finish with two buttons.

Adding twine to the bird's beak for a finishing touch really brings the scene to life. When the chicks hatch, she'll be bringing worms instead!

# home sweet home

That well known sentiment, 'There's no place like home', holds great meaning for us. When we started thinking about creating a lasting memory of the home, that little phrase kept coming back to us and formed the inspiration for this charming project. We worked primarily from photographs, translating these first into a painting and then a line drawing to encapsulate all of the details of the house. This doesn't have to be a true representation of your home. It could, like ours, be slightly romanticized with embroidered roses around the door and a garden full of pretty flowers.

Although there is some freehand machine embroidery and machine patchwork, the majority of this project is worked in hand appliqué and hand embroidery which makes this an ideal and enjoyable project to pick up and fit in around family life.

*Mid pleasures and palaces though we may roam,*
*Be it ever so humble, there's no place like home;*

JOHN HOWARD PAYNE

## You will need

- 50 x 50cm (20 x 20in) natural linen
- 50 x 50cm (20 x 20in) calico or muslin
- Embroidery hoop (30cm/12in diameter)
- Four strips of red/brown fabrics 2 x 120cm
  (¾ x 47in) for roof
- 10 x 30cm (4 x 12in) rust coloured fabric for
  terracotta shingles
- 15 x 30cm (5⅞ x 12in) textured white fabric
  for house
- White scraps for windows and porch
- Red check scraps for chimneys and porch roof
- Approx. 14 bright embroidery threads for flowers
  and leaves
- 30 x 20cm (12 x 8in) pale green organza for
  foliage and grass
- Straw needle
- Machine darning foot
- 30cm (12in) double-sided fusible webbing
  (Bondaweb)
- Mounting card 40 x 50cm (15¾ x 20in)
- Wooden picture frame 40 x 50cm (15¾ x 20in)
- Fabric spray adhesive

You'll find the templates for this project on pages
114 and embroidery stitches on page 109

## Prepare

*One* If you are designing your own house, take some photographs face on to the house. From these, draw or paint it with as much detail and accuracy as you can. Then, redraw the house in line so that you can break each part down into different colours. At this stage you can also have some fun adding to your picture, with flower borders, for example. Then choose the fabrics you want to represent your house.

*Two* To construct the house, start by preparing the fabric for the patchwork roof. Take your four strips of fabric and sew them together with a 5mm (³⁄₁₆in) s/a along the length so that you create a piece of horizontally striped fabric. Cut this into three equal pieces 40cm (15¾in) long. Sew these pieces together so that you now have a piece of fabric with 12 stripes on it. Press the seams flat. Now cut this into 10 strips 4cm (1½in) wide **(a)**. Take the first and second strip. Turn one upside-down so that the pattern alternates. Pin with r/s together, stitch and press. Carry on with each piece so that you end up with a jumbled-up patchwork for the tiles.

*a*

We worked from a photograph to produce first a detailed painting, then a more stylized line drawing of our house.

**Three** Take your rust coloured fabric for the terracotta shingles. We have allowed extra fabric all around for the machine embroidery process: the finished size needs to be 22.5 x 6cm (8⁷⁄₈ x 2⁷⁄₈in), including a 5mm (³⁄₈in) s/a. Using the darning foot attachment, drop the feed dog and thread with black sewing thread. Working from left to right, move across the fabric in continual U shapes of approximately 1cm (³⁄₈in) across. Guide the fabric gently. If you are too heavy handed, your shingles will look spiky! At the end of each row, cut off the threads. Start again at the left side, making sure that the point of the new row touches the circle of the row above. Continue until you have filled in the pattern shape. Don't worry if your embroidery is a bit uneven – it's meant to look rustic!

**Four** Cut out the base of the house from the white fabric 22.5 x 7.5cm (8⁷⁄₈ x 3in). Draft the patterns for the house (page 114), pin on to the fabrics and cut out. Draw the foliage and grass shapes on to Bondaweb (remember to reverse the image) and fuse to the green organza.

## Assemble the house

**One** Turn under all the edges of your house pieces and tack. Pin the roof, chimney stacks and pots, shingle and bottom house pieces into position on the linen background, tucking the left hand chimney inside the top edge of the roof. Hand sew in place using a slipstitch. Remove all the tackings.

**Two** Position the window, door and porch on to the house and hand sew in place using a slipstitch. Remove all the tackings and give the whole work a good press.

## Embroider

*One* Mount the whole piece on to the calico or muslin to give a bit more substance to the fabric for the embroidery. Mark out the window panes with tailors chalk. Fuse the foliage and grass pieces on to the front of the house. This gives a subtle background to embroider the flowers on to **(b)**.

*Two* Put the work in an embroidery hoop and you are ready to begin. All the embroidery is worked in two thread embroidery silk and we use straw or milliners needles, rather than crewel needles, as they are slim and sharp and, because they are long, they are easier to use for French knots or bullions.

b

### Design Inspiration

Take a look at your neighbourhood and design a larger picture which could include your home and all the everyday things that make your street interesting like the post box, trees, cats and dogs – even a bus going past!

Small details in backstitch really add to the rustic look.

**Window panes and windows:** embroider these first as some of your flowers will trail across the bottom panes. With a pale brown embroidery thread, satin stitch across each window pane. Don't worry if it isn't very even, this adds to the charm! With black thread, backstitch around the windows to give definition.

**Leafy foreground:** this creates the base from which all the flowers will follow. Start along the bottom line of the foliage and edge of the house. Take a length of green embroidery thread and sew a row of random chain stitches to suggest leaves.

**Door and porch:** with black thread, backstitch lines down the door and across the white triangle on the porch roof to suggest tongue and groove. Then with a small backstitch, embroider a door latch.

**Smoke:** add wisps of smoke to the top of one of your chimney pots with a small backstitch in two shades of grey.

**Rambling rose:** take a length of the green thread and stem stitch the windy stem of the rose around the porchway. In a selection of pinks, randomly embroider the bullion roses, which are made up of three rows of bullion stitches embroidered closely together.

### Keep control
Using an embroidery hoop keeps the fabric taut and controls the work whilst creating the hand embroidery.

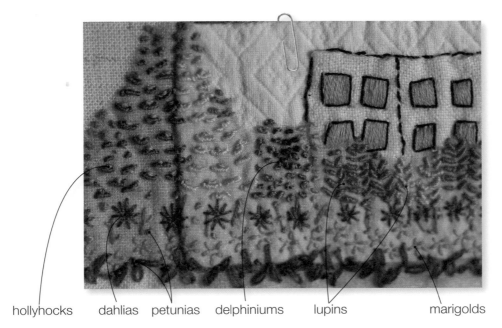

hollyhocks   dahlias   petunias   delphiniums   lupins   marigolds

**Marigolds:** using yellow thread, straight stitch little five-sided stars to create the marigolds. In a lighter green thread, make a series of different length straight stitches to give the illusion of flower stems.

**Delphiniums:** in shades of pale blue, purple and navy, make the delphinium shape by embroidering columns of French knots (three to a row) in varying heights.

**Hollyhocks:** start at the top of the column with pale green thread and embroider a few French knots. Working your way down, change to either a magenta or pink thread and embroider a few more French knots. Working your way down and out, change to bullion stitches so that at the bottom of the column you have a row of four or five bullion stitches. Highlight each bullion stitch with a yellow French knot.

**Lupins:** with combinations of pinks and reds, start at the top of the column with a French knot and then work your way down with rows of two diagonal bullion stitches mirroring each other.

**Dahlias:** choosing a soft red, straight stitch nine-sided stars. Make them a little larger than the marigolds.

**Petunias:** using pinks, yellows and purples, fill in any gaps in the embroidery with French knots.

## Finish

**One** Give your completed picture a final press under a pressing cloth. Working from the centre, mark out the border of your work so that it measures 34 x 44cm (13⅜ x 17¼in) and trim off all excess fabric. Press under 2cm (¾in) all the way round.

**Two** To help the work lie flat, mitre the corners as follows: open out the pressed seams at the corners and where the two foldlines meet, insert a pin. Make a crease diagonally at this point and score along the foldline with your fingernail. Refold the seams and pin into position at the mitres. Slipstitch into place.

**Three** Turn the work back to the front and sew a small running stitch in a natural coloured sewing thread just inside the edge. Give a final press and spray mount into position centrally on the mounting card. Place in the frame and hang.

# sweet dreams

What better way to end a busy day than to climb into a bed made up with luxurious, crisp cotton linen? With this in mind, we mixed the best quality organic percale cotton with a quirky appliqué flower, inspired by and made from once fashionable 1970's floral and abstract fabrics. This has created a wonderfully eye catching duvet and pillowcase set, perfect for a modern bedroom.

The accompanying quilted linen bag on page 34 is designed to store the duvet and pillowcases in and completes a lovely project to give as a very special gift or wedding present. This is a useful and fun way to use up your dated bed linens that have been stashed away in the linen cupboard for years.

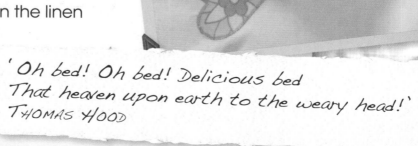

'Oh bed! Oh bed! Delicious bed
That heaven upon earth to the weary head!'
THOMAS HOOD

## You will need

**For the duvet cover:**

· 1 x 1m (39¼ x 39¼in) squared paper for drafting up

· 202 x 211cm (79½ x 83in) organic percale cotton (see supplier list page 126) for front

· 202 x 131cm (79½ x 51½in) organic percale cotton for back

· 10 mother-of-pearl buttons size 2cm (¾in) in pastel shades

· Five different 1970's retro or patterned pillowcases for outer flower petals

· Two scraps of retro fabric for flower centre

· Seven different coloured multipurpose sewing threads (each a shade darker than your fabrics to highlight)

**For each pillow case:**

· 50 x 50cm (20 x 20in) squared paper for drafting up

· 52 x 175cm (20½ x 69in) organic percale cotton

· Retro fabrics as duvet cover

· Sewing threads as duvet cover

· Five mother of pearl buttons size 2cm (¾in) in pastel shades

**For entire project:**

· 5m (196in) Double-sided fusible webbing (Bondaweb)

You'll find the templates for this project on pages 116–118

# Duvet cover

## Prepare

*One* Draw out the large appliqué flower design on to squared paper using the scaled-up templates (pages 116–118) and following the pattern below. Then use this drawing as both a guide and template from which to draft up the Bondaweb. On a pattern this precise, any slight error could cause the whole design to shift and become inaccurate so, if your shapes do not fit precisely, you can alter the design on your squared paper before drawing out the Bondaweb. Number each shape so that you know where each goes. Using your chart, draw out the Bondaweb, fuse on to your chosen retro fabrics and cut out. Using the medium heart template, draw out 48 hearts on to Bondaweb, fuse 12 of each on to four of your retro fabrics and cut out.

*Two* Take the duvet front piece. To create the button band, press under one shorter edge 5cm (2in) and then press under a further 5cm (2in). Pin and topstitch near to the inner folded edge and press. Along the button band, mark out 10 buttonholes starting 10cm (4in) in from both side edges and then at every 20cm (8in) interval. Make buttonholes referring to your sewing machine instructions.

*Three* Take the duvet back piece. Create the under-facing for the pillowcase detail by pressing under one shorter edge 10cm (4in) and then a further 10cm (4in). Pin and topstitch near to the inner folded edge and press.

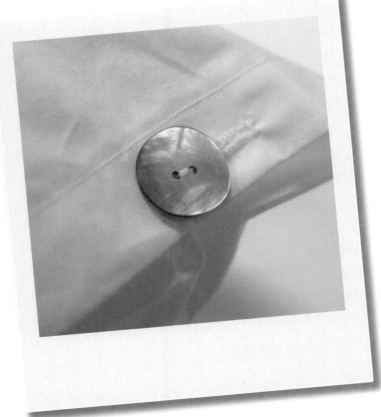

Hearts and flowers make
a dreamy combination and
herald a good night's sleep.

Mother-of-pearl buttons in colours to complement
your fabrics add to the sense of luxury.

## Add the appliqué

*One*  Take your chart to a large window and,
holding it up to the light, draw the outline of your
shapes on to the back of your paper to reverse
the design, also transferring your reference
numbers. Find the centre point on the duvet front
– this is where your first shape will be applied.
Following your reversed chart, carefully place all
your shapes on to the front of the duvet. Line up,
leaving no gaps, and fuse.

*Two*  Set your sewing machine to zigzag stitch,
width 3mm (1/8in), length 1mm (1/20in). Starting with
the outer shapes and working your way in, zigzag
(satin stitch) around each shape with a thread
of a darker matching shade to create an outline
and prevent the fabric from lifting up. Note that
the wide stitch width allows you to stitch over the
butted up edges of two different shapes.

*Three*  Take your hearts and scatter them
randomly around the outside of the flower, roughly
eight hearts per corner and four to each side of
the flower. Fuse and stitch around each shape,
again using your darker matching threads, with
your zigzag set to 2mm (3/32in) wide and 1mm
(1/20in) long.

## Finish the duvet

*One*  To make up the duvet, place the front and
back pieces r/s together with the under-facing
folded up over the bottom edge of the front by
10cm (4in). This creates the pillowcase finish.
Because of the volume of fabric to be stitched
and to prevent movement, carefully pin around all
edges including the under-facing. Stitch the two
side seams and the top seam. Clip the corners
and zigzag or overlock to finish. Turn through, sew
on the buttons and give a final press.

### Make the bed

To put your duvet cover on easily, first turn
the cover inside out. Place your hands into
the top two corners of the cover and grab two
corners of the duvet. Holding tightly, give it
a flick whilst turning the cover to the right
side. Push the duvet into the bottom two
corners and fasten the buttons.

# Pillowcase

## Prepare

*One*  Follow the preparation instructions for the duvet cover on page 30, but this time use the pattern below right and the pillowcase templates and remember you are only drafting up a chart for half the design. Draw up your Bondaweb and fuse to the retro fabrics as before. Using the smallest heart template, draw out 12 hearts on to the Bondaweb, fuse three of each on to your four retro fabrics and cut out.

*Two*  Take the pillowcase and press one short end under 2.5cm (1in) and then under a further 2.5cm (1in) to create the button band. Pin and topstitch near to the inner folded edge and press. Repeat with the other short end. With the w/s of the fabric facing you, measure along the long edge 75cm (29½in) from one end, fold over to create the front of the pillowcase and press. You still have an extra 15cm (6in) on the back half, which will form the under-facing and pillowcase finish.

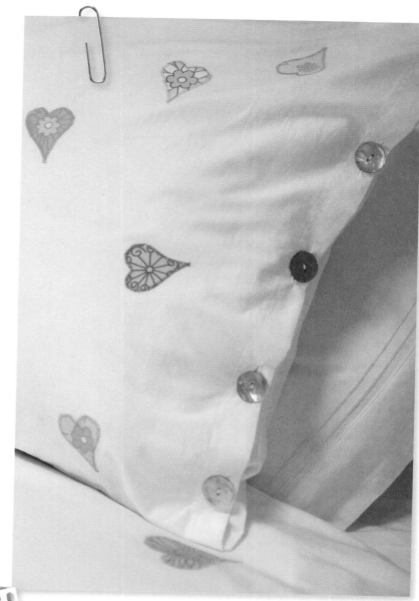

**Design Inspiration**
This project was inspired by a flower motif in one of the retro fabrics, but you could easily choose a selection of polka dot fabrics in different sizes and colours and appliqué them on to the duvet cover and pillowcases in a variety of circles.

Nestling together, the two pillowcases make a perfect pair. You could easily play around with the flower and heart designs to make a lovely version for a single bed.

*Follow your heart*
*When cutting out the heart shapes, look for interesting patterns within the fabrics that will look good within the heart shape (not too much of one colour). You will use more fabric but the results are worth it!*

It's great fun resurrecting these vintage bed linen fabrics but contemporary floral designs could also look stunning.

## Add the appliqué

*One* Take your chart to a large window and holding it up to the light, draw the outline of your shapes on to the back of your paper to reverse the design, also transferring your reference numbers. Working from the front of the pillow, with the folded edge to the right side, find your centre point along the fold. This is where you will start to position the appliqué. Using your chart and the pattern, left, as a guide, position the pieces and fuse. Complete the appliqué by following step two for adding the duvet appliqué (page 31).

*Two* Randomly place your hearts over the front. Fuse and stitch around each heart, again using your darker matching threads, with your zigzag set to 2mm (3/32in) wide and 1mm (1/20in) long.

## Finish the pillowcase

*One* On the front of the pillowcase, mark out five buttonholes along the button band, starting 5cm (2in) in from both side edges and then at 10cm (4in) intervals. Make buttonholes referring to your sewing machine instructions.

*Two* To create the pillowcase opening, place r/s together with the 15cm (6in) under-facing folded over the opening towards the front. Pin side seams and stitch. Clip the corners and zigzag or overlock to finish. Turn through, sew on the buttons and give a final press.

Repeat all pillowcase instructions to make a second pillowcase.

# lovely linen

Store your duvet cover and pillowcases in this luxurious quilted bag, made from the same percale cotton with retro appliqué hearts and a flower. Or why not make it for a child's room to keep a precious soft toy collection safe?

## You will need

- 42 x 122cm (16½ x 48in) organic percale cotton
- 42 x 122cm (16½ x 48in) 2oz wadding
- 42 x 122cm (16½ x 49in) cotton muslin for backing
- 42 x 122cm (16½ x 48in) silk for lining
- Two strips of silk 4 x 102cm (1½ x 40in) for ties
- Five different retro fabrics or pillowcases as for duvet cover
- Two 4 x 27cm (1½ x 10½in) retro fabric pieces for casings
- Sewing threads as for duvet cover
- Five embroidery threads to match fabrics
- Chalk pencil
- Sewing machine walking foot
- Safety pin

You'll find the templates for this project on pages 117–118

### Feeding time
A walking foot is an essential tool for machine quilting as it feeds all the layers through the machine evenly and helps to prevent puckering.

## Prepare

*One* Take the large heart template and draw 20 hearts on to the Bondaweb. Fuse on to your five retro pillowcases. Take the small flower and small centre shapes, draw two of each on to the Bondaweb and fuse to your retro fabrics.

*Two* Fold the cotton main fabric in half and press to create the folded bottom edge. Open out and on the front r/s, measure 5cm (2in) up from the fold and 2cm (¾in) in from each side edge and equally position your first five hearts. Measure 2cm (¾in) down from the top edge and 2cm (¾in) in from each side edge and fuse the next five hearts. Then, measure 18cm (7in) down from the top edge and 4cm (1½in) in from the right side edge and position your flower and fuse. Repeat on the back, positioning the shapes in a mirror image.

*Three* Using the small heart template, draw up on to a piece of card and cut out. Taking the chalk pencil and card heart, mark out 10 hearts randomly across the bag front and in mirror image, 10 hearts across the bag back.

## Appliqué and quilting

*One* Set your zigzag to 2mm (³⁄₃₂in) wide and 1mm (¹⁄₂₀in) long and stitch around the fabric hearts and the flower. With the muslin on the bottom, and your appliquéd fabric r/s up on top, sandwich the wadding between them. The wadding will be 1cm (⅜in) shorter than both top edges. Baste a line of tacking down the centre front and three lines of tacking across to hold all layers in place. Stitch around the outside edge, just inside the seam line, with a small tacking stitch.

*Two* In the complementary embroidery threads, sew around the chalked hearts with a small running stitch to quilt (approx two stitches per cm/¾in) and then around the larger appliquéd hearts and flower **(a)**.

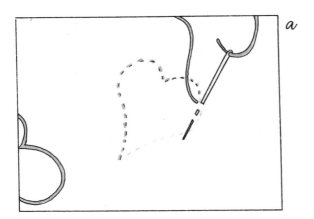

*a*

## Make up the bag

*One* With r/s together, pin the top edges of the top fabric to the lining (the wadding should finish just under the stitching line) and stitch. Fold the top fabric and joined lining in half r/s together, making sure that the top edge seams match up. Pin and stitch side seams using your walking foot, leaving a 15cm (6in) gap in the lining to turn through.

*Two* Remove all tacking and trim back the wadding and muslin along the seams to 2mm (³⁄₃₂in) to reduce the bulk. Turn through, sew up the gap in the lining and press carefully.

*Three* Turn under each short edge of casing 1cm (⅜in) and stitch. Then, turn under each long edge by 5mm (³⁄₁₆in) and press. Repeat with second casing piece. On the bag front and back, measure 11cm (4¼in) down from the top edge. Pin and tack the casing through the top fabric and lining. Sew the two long edges carefully to avoid puckering **(b)**. Repeat on the other side.

*b*

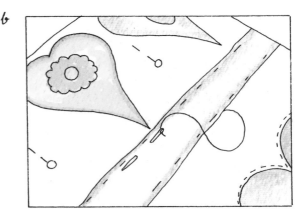

*Four* Take one tie. Turn under each short edge 1cm (⅜in) and press. Fold the long edges in half r/s together and, with the general-purpose foot on your machine, stitch with 1cm (⅜in) s/a. Trim back to 5mm (³⁄₁₆in) and turn through with a safety pin. Repeat with the second tie. Press.

*Five* To insert the drawstring, pin the safety pin on to one end of a tie and starting from the left hand side, thread through the front and back casing and tie each end in a knot. Take the second tie and repeat from the right hand side. Give the bag a final press.

# vintage flowers

A peaceful lie-in at the weekend, followed by breakfast in bed with a strong mug of coffee or a steaming cup of tea, brought on a tray with a softly boiled egg and buttery toasted 'soldiers' is always a blissful start to the day.

Taking inspiration from roses and 1930's table linen, we have designed a pretty tea cosy made from a felted wool jumper and colourfully embroidered with lazy daisies. The top is covered with roses made from pastel, floral-printed cottons and the finished cosy fits snugly over the pot. We have also designed a cafetière cosy in the same felted wool, embroidered with the lazy daisies and finished with printed cotton patchwork ties. A tray cloth, napkins and sweet egg cosy with lazy daisies, topped with a fabric rose, complete the set.

'Polly put the kettle on,
Polly put the kettle on,
Polly put the kettle on,
We'll all have tea.'
18th CENTURY NURSERY RHYME

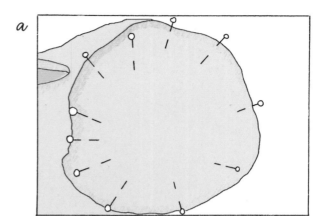
a

## You will need

- One large 100% pure wool, plain knit jumper
- Variety of pastel, floral print cottons 20 x 30cm (8 x 11¾in). Approx. 20 or double up
- Eight complementary embroidery threads
- 20 x 20cm (8 x 8in) square of wool felt for leaves
- One skein tapestry wool to contrast with jumper
- For tray cloth: 44 x 32cm (17¼ x 12½in) ivory linen
- For each napkin: 28 x 28cm (11 x 11in) ivory linen
- Transfer pencil

You'll find the templates for this project on pages 120–121

# Tea cosy

**One** Before starting this project you will need to felt the jumper, which must be made from 100 per cent wool. Some wools work better than others so there is some trial and error involved. As a general rule, put your jumper in the washing machine on the hottest cycle and the fastest spin cycle. Then, if possible, tumble dry. Repeat once or twice if necessary.

**Two** Draft up the pattern (pages 120–121), cut out all pieces from the felted jumper and add markings. The cosy has a double layer of wool to give greater insulation so the wool forms both the top fabric and lining fabric on this project. Take the two side panels and stitch r/s together between markings using zigzag stitch set to 1mm (1/20in) wide /2.5mm (1/10in) long, which will give a slight stretch to the stitch. Repeat with the lining pieces. Press open the seams. Pin pleats and stitch into position. Take the top circular piece and pin carefully to the side panels **(a)**. Because this is a jersey fabric there will be a lot of ease, so take your time when stitching. Clip and trim.

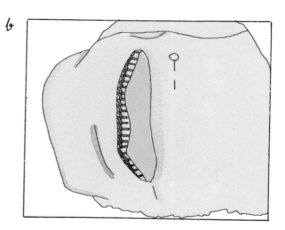
b

**Three** Repeat the above with the lining. Press open the seams. Insert the lining w/s together and pin the side openings. Leave the bottom open for now. Using the tapestry wool, stitch around the side openings with a large blanket stitch **(b)**. Turn through and turn up the bottom edge 1cm (3/8in), pin and blanket stitch.

**Four** Draw out the lazy daisy design (page 120) on to tracing paper with a transfer pencil. Press on to the side of the cosy to mark out the design. Repeat this process on the other side. Embroider each lazy daisy and French knot centre in a different colour to complement the rose fabrics. Use stem and chain stitches for the leaf and stem detail.

38 *Vintage Flowers*

## Make the roses

*One* There are many methods for making fabric roses but here's how we do it! To make bias-cut flowers you will need a selection of floral cottons in small prints (approx 20). If you don't have that many, just double up or you could do them all in one print. Pin the large and small rose pattern pieces (page 121) on to the bias of your fabrics. If it is a scrap of fabric and you are unsure where the bias is, move it around and pull at either end until you find the place where it has the greatest stretch. This will be the bias. Cut out approx. ten large and ten small. Fold along the long edge, r/s together and stitch both ends, turn through and press **(c)**.

*Two* Take a length of thread and at one raw edge start turning the fabric, quite tightly, pleating and taking a small stitch. Work around and around, tweaking the fabric to suggest a rose shape. When you get to the end, turn the point of the fabric over the raw edge to neaten **(d)**. This does take some practise so have a go with some scrap fabric first and remember, it's just an impression of a rose!

*Three* To apply the roses, take one at a time (larger ones first) and starting at the middle of the top of the cosy, pin and stitch around the rose with a tiny overstitch, enclosing any raw edge you may have. Work your way out, applying smaller ones to the outside edge. If the roses look like they might unravel a bit, put a final stitch through the centre of the rose and into the back of the cosy (you may need a thimble for this).

*Four* To finish, cut around the 12 leaves in wool felt and scatter around the edge of the roses. Sew down the middle of the leaf with a backstitch in a complementary thread to give a vein effect. Give the cosy a final press.

c

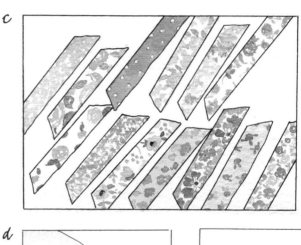

d

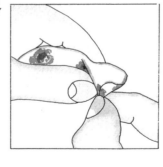
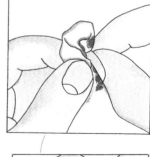
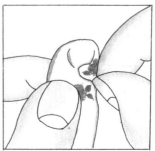
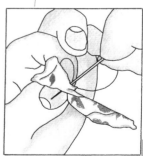

Floral cottons in small prints make stunning little roses but you could use plain cottons in colours from your garden for a bolder style.

# Cafetière cosy

**One** Cut out two pieces of felted wool (see tea cosy instructions, step 1, page 38) 33 x 16.5cm (13 x 6½in). Use the top of a cotton reel to curve the corners. R/S together, sew round the edges using a zigzag stitch 1mm (¹⁄₂₀in) wide /2.5mm (¹⁄₁₀in) long, leaving a gap to turn through. Clip and trim back seams. Turn through and hover steam from an iron over the seams, rolling between your fingers to open out fully. Press. Pin up the opening and blanket stitch all the way around the outer edge using the complementary tapestry wool.

**Two** Mark out your lazy daisy design (page 120) on a piece of tracing paper and outline with the transfer pencil. Press on to the fabric to mark out the design. Add the embroidered detail (see tea cosy instructions, page 38).

## Draw it out

As an alternative to our embroidery design, take inspiration from your own vintage tablecloth. Take a section that you like and work out an overall design by cutting a window out of a piece of paper and placing it over the design. You can then either trace or photocopy this section and then add bits in, or mirror image it to get a repeat.

## Design Inspiration

Why not use a felted Aran jumper for the tea, cafetière and egg cosies, decorated with butterflies, bees, ladybirds and big felt flowers? These motifs would also look fun translated into hand-stitched appliqué on the tray cloth and napkins.

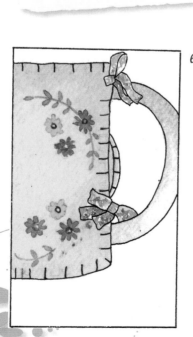

*e*

**Three** To make the ties, take the remaining binding (see tray cloth instructions, page 42). Fold in half and sew 5mm (³⁄₁₆in) from edge. Turn through with a safety pin. Take your time as you will have the bulk of all the seams to pull through so it is a bit fiddly. Press and cut into four strips 19cm (7½in) long and sew into position on the cosy **(e)**.

Bring some warmth to breakfast with a hot pot of coffee and an egg just waiting to be cracked open and dipped with toast.

# Egg cosy

*One*  Draft up the pattern (page 121) and cut out using the rib edging of the felted jumper as your bottom edge. It will taper in slightly but the rib stretches to fit snugly over the egg and egg cup. Sew all four pieces r/s together. Press the seams, clip and turn through. Using the small pattern for the fabric rose, make up a rose and sew on to the top (see tea cosy, page 39 for rose instructions). Sew lazy daisies with French knot centres randomly around the sides in complementary threads.

The lazy daisy theme ties our breakfast set together but take inspiration from embroidery on any vintage linen you may have.

# Tray cloth

*One*  Draft up the tray cloth dimensions on to plain paper (the dimensions given in the You Will Need list on page 38 are for our tray but you may need to adapt this slightly for yours). Mark out your embroidery using the tea cosy template (page 120) and illustration **g** for inspiration. If using your own design, start with your outer border and position this 3cm (1⅛in) in from the outside edge. Find your centre point and work out your design to give a balanced effect at the sides and the top and bottom. We have used a lazy daisy theme, but you could choose anything, such as strawberries or cups and saucers. Using a transfer pencil, copy your design on to tracing paper and press on to fabric to mark out the design. Embroider all the flowers in colours to complement the tea and cafetière cosies.

*Two*  To make the binding, take nine pieces of the floral printed cotton and cut out two of each piece, measuring 5 x 12cm (2 x 4¾in) strips. Place the strips so you are happy with the effect and sew r/s together along the long edge of each strip until you have a piece of fabric measuring 56 x 12cm (22 x 4¾in). Press seams open. Cut the fabric into four strips, each measuring 56 x 3cm (22 x 1⅛in). Sew the four lengths together to give a total of 216cm (85in). You now have your binding ready to attach **(f)**.

*Three*  Pin r/s binding to r/s tray cloth on one long edge. Cut off the surplus binding and machine stitch (5mm/³⁄₁₆in s/a). Repeat along the other long edge. Press binding open, repeat with the shorter edges. Press and turn binding over to w/s of tray cloth and turn under 5mm (³⁄₁₆in). Pin and slipstitch to finish **(g)**.

*f*

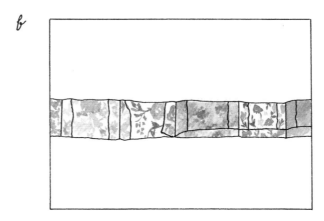

*g*

# Napkins

*One*  To ensure you are cutting out the napkins along the straight grain, pull out a thread from your linen and use this as a guide to cut along. Stitch 2cm (¾in) inside the edge of each side, using a 1mm wide/1mm long (¹⁄₂₀in) zigzag to prevent further fraying of the fabric. Draw the design (page 120) on to tracing paper with the transfer pencil and press to mark out the design on one corner of the napkin. Embroider the flowers with lazy daisies and fill the centres with bullion stitches. To finish, fray the edges by approx. 1.5cm (⅝in).

Charming and simple to make, the napkin and tray cloth bring a touch of 1930s elegance into your home.

# strawberries & cream

Picnics at any time of the year are great fun. It's strange how even simple, everyday fare tastes so much nicer out of doors! Strawberries are a firm favourite with both of our families, which is why we chose these delicious fruits as the inspiration for this mouth-watering picnic blanket.

Made from a beautiful, dusty pink, vintage wool blanket, the strawberries stencilled in the central panel are inspired by wood cut prints. Around the outer border are twelve appliquéd strawberries in a variety of pink and red prints. To make the blanket damp proof and to give a jaunty finish, the backing and border is finished with a red and white polka dot oilcloth.

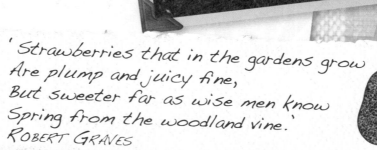

'Strawberries that in the gardens grow
Are plump and juicy fine,
But sweeter far as wise men know
Spring from the woodland vine.'
ROBERT GRAVES

## You will need

- One vintage wool blanket
- 12 pieces of red/pink printed fabric approx. 20 x 20cm (8 x 8in)
- 50cm (20in) green fabric for the stalks
- One A4 sheet of acetate
- Stencil brush
- Red, green and black fabric paint
- 180 x 130cm (71 x 51in) red/white polka dot oilcloth
- Sharp, fine blade craft knife
- Cutting mat
- Double-sided fusible webbing (Bondaweb)
- Fabric spray adhesive
- An extra pair of hands

You'll find the templates for this project on page 115

## Prepare

*One* From the blanket, cut out one centre panel 94 x 54cm (37 x 21¼in), two short side panels 35 x 54cm (13¾ x 21¼in) and two long side panels 35 x 160cm (13¾ x 63in).

*Two* Draft up the templates on page 115 for the strawberry, stalk and outline stencils and, using the craft knife, cut out from the acetate. To achieve this, tape the motif to the cutting mat and then tape the acetate over the top to prevent movement whilst cutting out.

*Three* Find the centre point on the centre panel. This will be where you place your first strawberry motif stencil. Before starting, we recommend that you take time to work out where you want to position each strawberry to create a balanced design. To do this, either draw or photocopy approx. 24 of your strawberry motifs on to some scrap paper. Cut them out and place them on the centre panel so that you can decide where to position your stencils. You might have to move them around for a while to achieve a nice effect. We decided to place the strawberries randomly but you may wish to print them in one direction. Pin them down and lift off one at a time to do each stencil **(a)**.

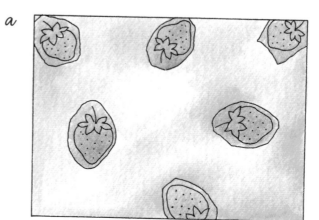

*a*

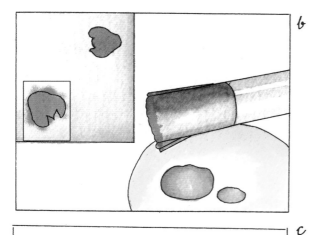

b

c

## Stencil the strawberries

*One*   Starting with the main strawberry stencil (red), lightly spray the reverse with fabric adhesive spray to prevent it from moving whilst stencilling. Pour out some of the fabric paint on to an old plate and dunk the tip only of the stencil brush into the paint. Dab off the excess on to a scrap of paper and apply the paint to the fabric using an up and down movement with the brush. Make sure that the stencil has an equal covering of the paint and then repeat on all the other strawberries **(b)**.

*Two*   Let the paint dry thoroughly and then apply the leaf motif and finally the black outline **(c)**. Be careful not to overload the brush with paint as this will make the stencil bleed. To finish, press under a cloth to make the dye colourfast following the manufacturer's instructions.

The instant results of stencilling on fabric make it so satisfying. Practise on some scraps before you go for the real thing.

## Sew the panels

**One** Take one of the short side panels and pin to the short side of the centre panel r/s together and stitch. Repeat with the other side. Press the seams outwards. Now, r/s together, pin and stitch the two long side panels to either side of the side and centre panels. Press the seams outwards. In a complementary colour, topstitch all the seams. You now have a centre and outer panel.

### Pressing matters
Under no circumstances should you use an iron with oilcloth – you will get into a terrible mess as the heat could melt the coating. We recommend that you score all edges with your thumbnail instead of pressing with an iron.

### Design Inspiration
There really are endless possibilities for this picnic blanket. You could print and appliqué an item of picnic food all over it, or perhaps a shell, starfish, fish, crab or other seaside creature. Or what about woodland animals like rabbits and squirrels?

## Add the appliqué

**One** Draw out 12 of the large strawberries on to Bondaweb, fuse on to your red and pink printed fabrics and cut out. Repeat with the green stalks.

**Two** Place the motifs around what is now the outer panel of the blanket at even intervals and fuse into position. Remember to allow for the 4cm (1½in) oilcloth border, so ensure that the strawberries finish at least 8cm (3⅛in) from the outside edge. Machine appliqué around the strawberries.

Plump and juicy, the appliquéd strawberries look good enough to eat.

The cheerful oilcloth backing will keep your picnic party and your feast comfortably dry if the ground is damp with dew.

## Back with oilcloth

*One* On a clean floor (you need the space) lay out your oilcloth w/s up. Take the back of your blanket and evenly cover with fabric spray adhesive. With the help of a friend, lay it out w/s together, centrally on top of the oilcloth. Smooth out all creases and pin around the central panel. Trim back the edges of the oilcloth to 6cm (2⅜in) **(d)**.

*Two* Turn under 2cm (¾in) using your thumbnail to press the oilcloth **(e)**. Turn under another 4cm (1½in) and pin. Topstitch around the centre panel of the blanket in a red thread to prevent the two fabrics from bagging. Finally, topstitch around the outer edge of the oilcloth to give a firm edge and decorative finish.

d

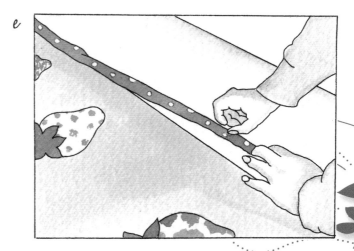

e

# garden game

With the summer holidays in full swing, many of our days are spent in the garden. Unfortunately, sometimes 'rain stops play', so it's back indoors and out with the games. Snakes and ladders has always been a firm favourite with our kids, which led us to design a floor quilt as a fun variation on the traditional game. It's perfect for playing inside and outdoors! Taking inspiration from the garden, there are roses to climb up, garden creatures to slide down, and one snake for extra excitement.

To accompany the game, there are four, three-dimensional counters, hand embroidered with a butterfly, ladybird, spider and bumble bee and a large, colourful, fabric dice. The background is a simple patchwork with the appliquéd flowers and creatures stitched through all layers to give a pleasing quilted effect. This is sure to give years of enjoyment to your family.

'Rain rain go away,
Come again another day.'

TRADITIONAL NURSERY RHYME

## You will need

- 1m x 150cm (39¼ x 59in) black and white ticking for patchwork
- 1m x 150cm (39¼ x 59in) cream linen for patchwork
- 135 x 135cm (53 x 53in) wadding
- 135 x 135cm (53 x 53in) lightweight calico for mounting
- 160 x 140cm (63 x 55in) green cotton for quilt backing, fabric and ties
- 50 x 140cm (20 x 55in) green printed cotton for the binding
- 30 x 30cm (12 x 12in) white felt for numbers
- 25cm (10in) each of yellow, grey, red and lavender felt for the counters and dice
- Black embroidery thread for the numbers and the counters
- Various colours of complementary multipurpose sewing threads for the appliqué
- Various colours of complementary embroidery threads for the quilting and details
- 1m (39¼in) green cotton fabric for flower stems
- Six different coloured scraps of floral cottons for the flower heads
- Six different coloured scraps of plain cottons or linens for the flower centres to complement the florals
- Pink and red cotton fabrics for the worms
- Natural and brown fabrics for the centipede and millipede
- Warm brown and gold fabric for the adder
- Lime green fabric for the caterpillar
- 2m (78½in) double-sided fusible webbing (Bondaweb)
- Chalk pencil or quilter's pencil
- Fabric adhesive spray
- Tear-away stabiliser (Stitch and Tear)
- Toy stuffing

You'll find the templates for this project on pages 122–123

**Unless otherwise stated all measurements in this project include a 1cm s/a**

## Make the patchwork

*One*   Cut 32 squares of ticking and 32 squares of cream linen, 18 x 18cm (7 x 7in). To create the patchwork base of eight by eight squares, lay out the patchwork pieces with the ticking running horizontally and alternate ticking and plain fabric. Working vertically, take the first eight squares and with r/s together pin and stitch. Press the seams open, turn and press from the right side. Repeat with the rest of the squares. You now have eight vertical strips. Press all the seams.

*Two*   Pin two of the vertical strips r/s together ensuring that all the seam lines match up. Stitch, press the seams open and repeat until all the strips are sewn together to create the patchwork checkerboard base of your quilt.

*Three*   Cut out 64 squares in white felt, each 2 x 2cm (¾ x ¾in). Draw numbers 1–64 on to tear-away stabiliser (Stitch and Tear) and pin and backstitch in black embroidery thread on to the squares. Tear away carefully and lay each felt square on to each patchwork square, referring to the plan opposite for positioning. Hold down each felt square with a running stitch using a green embroidery thread. Make sure that the numbers on the outside squares are at least 2cm (¾in) in from the edge.

### Design Inspiration

The basis of this quilt using the checkerboard design would translate perfectly into other board games like chess or drafts. Choose white and black fabric to create your squares and then embroider the counters with the king, queen, bishops, knights, rooks and pawns. These could be turned upside down to play drafts.

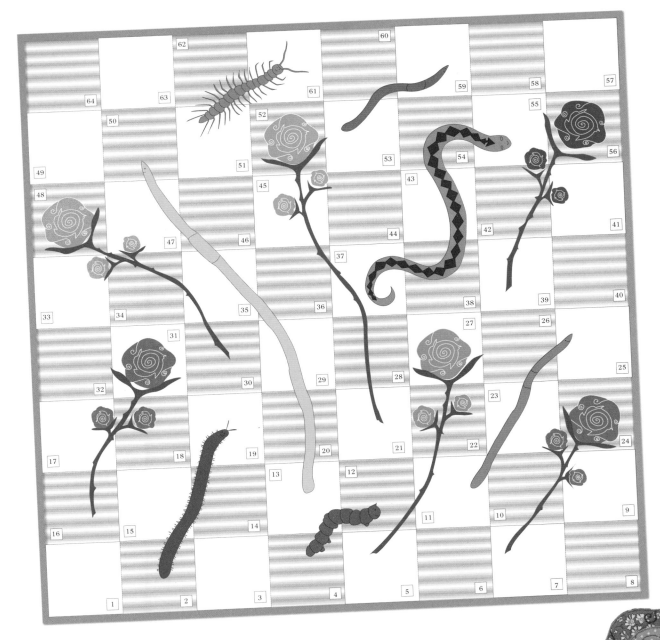

## Add the appliqué

*One*  Draw out a pattern of the whole quilt on to graph paper, 8 x 8 rows, with each square 16 x 16cm (6¼ x 6¼in). Scale up the flower and creature templates and extend the flower stems down to the relevant numbers squares, using the plan above as a pattern. Make templates for the three worms, using our images as inspiration. Reverse and draw all these out on to Bondaweb, fuse on to your chosen fabrics and cut out. Lay the patchwork on to a large, clean, flat surface, on top of a few thick blankets as a temporary ironing surface. Take the flower stems and heads, peel off the back of the Bondaweb, place on the quilt referring to the plan above for positioning and fuse under a pressing cloth. Insert a quilter's pin into the centre of each flower to keep in position whilst sewing.

*Two*  Select your sewing and embroidery thread colours. We have used colours to complement our flowers, but have swapped them all round to create contrast and definition. Using a matching thread, machine appliqué the stems. Then, with your chosen contrasting thread, machine appliqué the flower heads and flower centres.

**Three** Peel off the backing of the Bondaweb creatures and place on to the quilt, referring to the design layout, and fuse as before. Then, choose your sewing and embroidery threads and machine appliqué. Press well.

*Roll it up*

As the quilt top is very large, you will need to fold or roll your fabric both horizontally and vertically before proceeding with the machine appliqué so the bulk of the fabric moves more easily through the arm of the machine. Hold your fabric roll in place with a couple of safety pins.

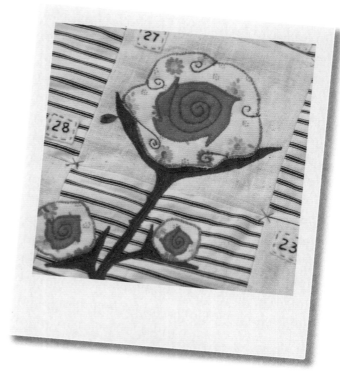

The inspiration for our flower shape came from a little watercolour painting. Photos, magazine clippings, fabric designs and even decorative china can all provide ideas for appliqué.

## Quilt

**One** To stabilize the work and prepare it for quilting, take the wadding and place it on a flat surface. Spray some fabric adhesive on to the wadding, gently place the calico mounting fabric on top and smooth out from the centre. Turn over so that the wadding is now facing up and again spray the surface lightly with the fabric adhesive. Place the pressed patchwork front on top, smoothing out from the centre as before. Pin to hold in place and now, from the centre out, baste through all layers as illustrated to hold the work in place **(a)**. Stitch a 1cm (⅜in) running stitch just inside the s/a all around the outside edge.

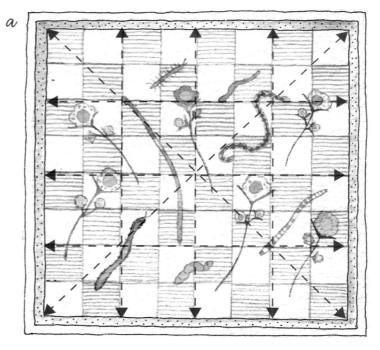

**Two** Referring to your templates, transfer all the details on to your flowers and creatures, either drawing freehand with a chalk or quilter's pencil or by your preferred method. Take the embroidery thread and stitch through all layers with backstitch down the centre of the flower stems and around the flower details **(b)**.

**Three** Using a running stitch, quilt around all the creatures except the centipede (which needs stitching across each segment) and add the leg, face and antennae details with backstitch. Folding the work whilst quilting allows you to move the quilt around more easily as you stitch.

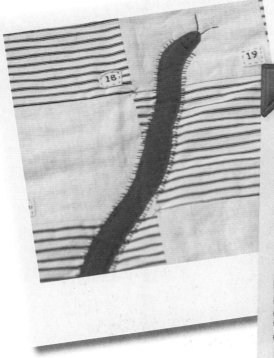

It takes a little time to stitch but children love the creepy crawly centipede.

The dice falls on number 55 and … bad luck, the counter slithers all the way back down to 37.

## Add fabric ties, backing and binding

*One* Adding the ties means the quilt can be neatly rolled up and put away when not in use. Cut two strips 10 x 138cm (4 x 54¼in) from green backing fabric. With r/s together, fold in half along the long edge and stitch leaving the ends open. Turn through, press, tuck the raw edges inside and topstitch all four sides. Repeat with the second strip. Cut out the backing fabric 135 x 135cm (53 x 53in). Position the straps on to this as shown in the diagram **(c)**, pin and stitch a 14cm (5½in) rectangle in the centre to fix in place.

*Two* Lay the backing cloth w/s up on a flat surface, lightly spray with fabric adhesive and position the quilt r/s up on top. Smooth out and pin from the centre. With a small running stitch, sew all the layers together around the outside edge, just inside the 1cm (⅜in) s/ a. Trim back the wadding, calico mounting fabric and backing fabric so that it is 1cm (⅜in) larger all around than the outside of the quilt edge.

*Three* For the binding, take your green printed cotton and cut two strips 6 x 135cms (2⅜ x 53in) and two strips 6 x 145cm (2⅜ x 57in) – these measurements are generous to allow for error. Press all strips in half along the length, w/s together, to create a crisp final edge, then open them out. Take one of the shorter strips and pin and stitch the binding to the quilt edge (not the wadding edge) r/s together. Repeat on the opposite side of the quilt. Cut off any surplus. Gently press the binding up, taking care not to flatten the wadding. Repeat with the longer edges. Press and turn the binding over all the layers towards the backing. Turn under 1cm (⅜in). Pin and slipstitch to finish.

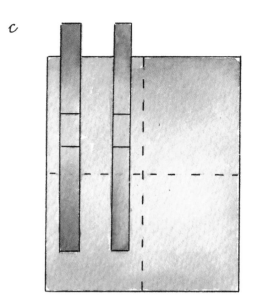

*c*

Small hands will have wonderful fun with this colourful dice – they can use it for all their other games, too.

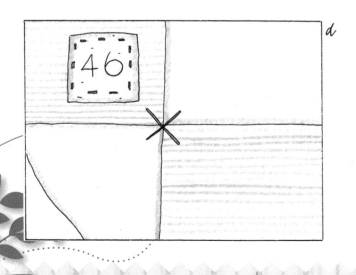

*d*

*Four* Finish off the quilt by making a cross-stitch in green embroidery thread (split to two threads) at all corner points that are not covered with appliqué. Stitch through all the layers ensuring that the reverse is neat and shows two small regular lines **(d)**.

## Make the counters

*One* Make a paper pattern of a round counter 13cm (5in) diameter and a strip 40 x 4cm (15¾ x 1½in). Cut out two circles and one strip from each of your four different coloured felts. Draw your designs using the templates on page 122 on to Stitch and Tear. Pin on to the top circle of felt and backstitch the detail with black embroidery thread. Carefully tear off **(e)**. Both the herringbone detail on the spider, bee and butterfly and the French knots on the ladybird will need to be applied after the Stitch and Tear is removed.

*Two* Take the felt strip and stitch the short ends together. Pin the strip and circle r/s together all the way round the top and bottom, leaving a 5cm (2in) opening for turning through and stuffing on the bottom edge. Stitch, taking care not to pleat the fabric. Clip, turn through, stuff firmly and close the opening with a slipstitch. Repeat for all counters **(f)**.

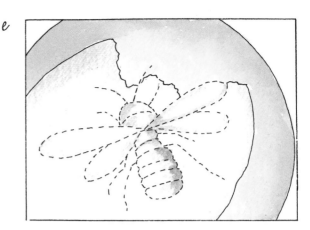

*e*

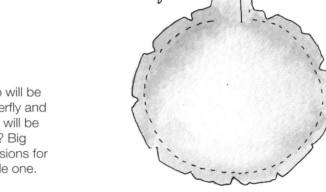

*f*

Who will be butterfly and who will be bee? Big decisions for a little one.

## Make the dice

*One* Cut out six squares, 12 x 12cm (4¾ x 4¾in), in six different coloured felts. Reverse the colour of the spots for opposite squares. Draw out 21 spots 2.5cm (1in) diameter on to Bondaweb. Fuse one in yellow felt, two in grey, three in red, four in green, five in white and six in lilac. Fuse on to the squares and overstitch around each spot with a complementary embroidery thread.

*Two* Lay numbers four, five and three side by side. With r/s together pin and stitch the seams starting and ending 1cm (⅜in) in from the end. Press the seams open. Repeat this process to sew square number six to square number two. Next stitch square number one to square number five, and then number five to number six. This will create a cross shape **(g)**. With r/s together, sew up all edges leaving a gap in the final edge. Turn through the gap, stuff firmly and close the opening with a slipstitch.

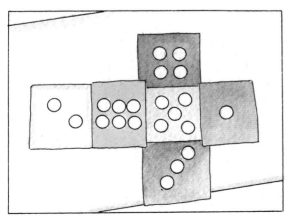

*g*

# rags to riches

In our studios, we always have a basket overflowing with scraps but we rarely have found a use for old T-shirts. Throughout the world, generations of families have taken part in the craft of rag rugging, using fabrics from clothing that was too worn to mend. What better way to use up those old T-shirts?

The warmth of the colours found on a bright autumn or fall day never fail to inspire us. These magnificent, earthy tones led us to choose rich colours for this stunning rag rug. We have kept the rug simple using a geometric design that allows the colours of our T-shirts to shine through. Tactile and soft, it will welcome you into your home on even the darkest of days.

'I know I'd go from rags to riches
If you would only say you cared,
And though my pockets may be empty
I'd be a millionnaire.'
ELVIS PRESLEY

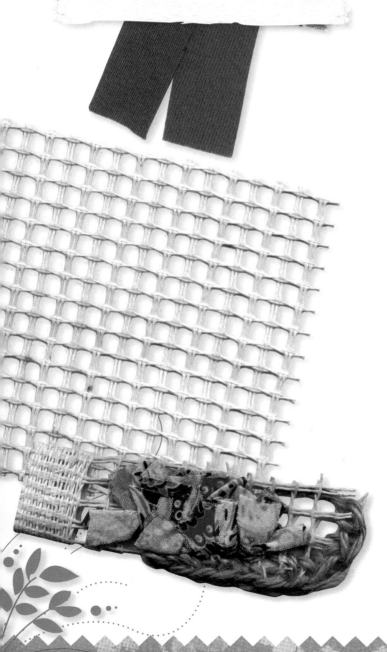

## You will need

- 20 to 25 T-shirts in a variety of different colours (the larger the better)
- 70 x 50cm (27½ x 20in) 3.3 hpi (holes per inch) rug canvas (finished rug size approximately 60 x 40cm/23½ x 15½in)
- 70 x 50cm (27½ x 20in) hessian for backing
- Chalk pencil
- Latch hook
- Sisal twine
- Crochet hook size 5 (UK)
- Squared pattern paper
- Coloured pencils

## Sourcing your T-shirts

*One* Many of us have slightly worn or outgrown T-shirts sitting in the cupboard just waiting to be reused and some may be perfect to put into your own rag rug. Even a small rug will use quite a few T-shirts. Adult T-shirts with long sleeves will give you more fabric strips, though don't disregard children's ones as these are good for small areas and highlights. Plain colours give a strong overall effect but prints can also be used. Bear in mind, though, that the reverse is usually plain and of a lighter colour, which can give more texture and a pleasing random effect. If you only have a few T-shirts to hand, ask friends and family for their cast-offs and look in your local thrift store to build up a good pile of interesting colours.

## Prepare the canvas

*One* To prepare your canvas for ragging, first you will need to make a firm neat edge. Allow an extra 5cm (2in) around the outside and cut out. Check that you have the desired rows and columns for your design (in our case 80 squares by 53 squares).

*Two* Fold under your hem approx. 5cm (2in) along each edge and stitch down to secure well, ensuring that all the holes remain open, and match up. This can be done by hand or on the machine as you prefer, but it is essential that it is accurate. For larger rugs, a wooden frame is often used to keep control of the canvas and to help keep its shape, but you can easily create this small rug without one.

## Design the rug

*One* To design your rug, first draw out a rectangle on to squared paper, 80 x 53 squares. Using coloured pencils, plan out your design, remembering that the knots are created on the horizontal lines of your canvas and not within the holes. You can scale up the design we have charted opposite or have fun designing your own arrangement of colours, based on the T-shirts you have sourced. Once you are happy with your design, transfer this on to your prepared rug canvas using the coloured pencils.

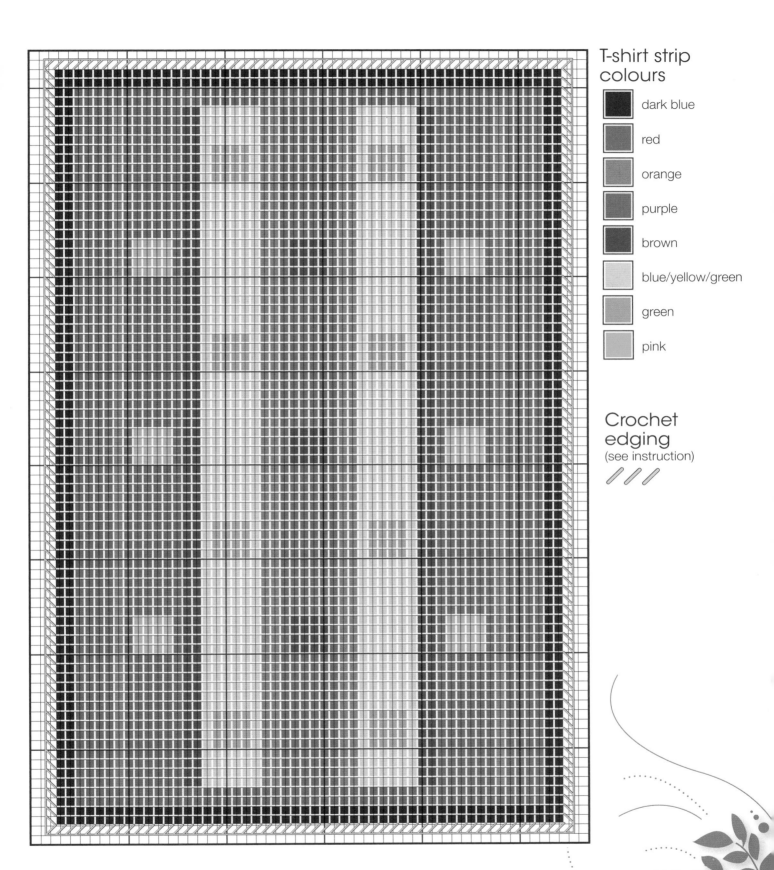

## T-shirt strip colours

- dark blue
- red
- orange
- purple
- brown
- blue/yellow/green
- green
- pink

## Crochet edging
(see instruction)

## Cut the strips

*One* The best T-shirts for ragging are the softer, lightweight ones as they pull very easily through the rug canvas. Heavyweight jerseys should be avoided, but medium-weight ones can be used and should be cut into slightly thinner strips (minimum 1cm/⅜in). Ensure that your T-shirts are clean and prepare them by cutting them into large, workable pieces. First, cut off the sleeves at the armhole and cut up the underarm seam. Separate the front and the back by cutting at all the seam lines. Trim off any s/a and hems and press well.

*Two* This should leave you with four flat pieces of fabric to mark up and cut out, the two opened sleeves plus the front and back. Most T-shirts will have more stretch in one direction, across the rib, which usually goes around the body on the garment. Carefully check this, as your strips need to be cut from the lesser stretch, which goes along the length of the rib. This will prevent fraying and stretching. Practise on a small sample of the sleeve before cutting your main strips in order to find the correct direction to cut.

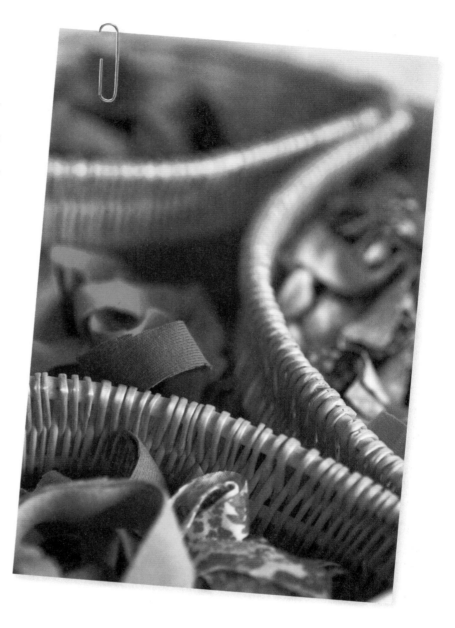

### Sorting strips
Cutting can be hard work on the hands so put aside a little time for prepping your strips. Separate them into bags or baskets in groups of colours.

*Three* Measure up from the bottom straight edge and mark 11cm (4¼in) with chalk. Repeat until you have a few strips all 11cm (4¼in) wide. Now, straighten any wonky ends and cut out your strips. You can do this by eye but it helps to place your work on a cutting mat, which has grid lines that you can follow. Your strips need to be about 1.5cm (⅝in) wide. You can cut your fabric doubled to save time.

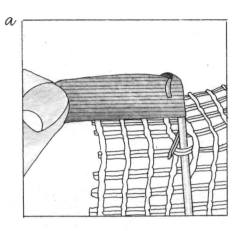

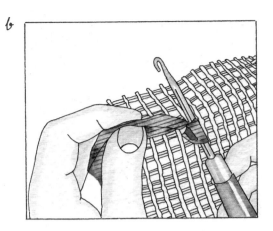

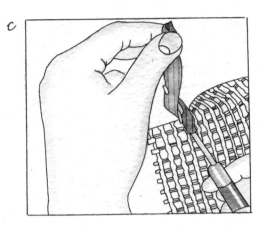

## Make the knots

Our rug is based upon a clip or peg rug. Traditionally these were created using a prodder tool, however we have used a latch hook tool to 'hook' or 'knot' our rug in a similar fashion to a hooked wool yarn rug. There are a couple of different methods of creating the knots but we are going to show you the five-step method, which we find more suitable for pulling through fabric strips.

*One*  Insert the latch hook tool through a square of canvas and up through the one above. With the hook open, catch the loop of a folded strip **(a)**.

*Two*  Holding on to the ends of the strip, pull the hook until the loop of fabric goes through both holes in the canvas **(b)**.

*Three*  Push your tool back through the loop of fabric ensuring that the hook is open.

*Four*  Place both ends of the strip into the open hook **(c)**.

*Five*  Pull the hook back through the loop to create the knot, gently tugging the two ends of the strip to tighten the knot **(d)**.

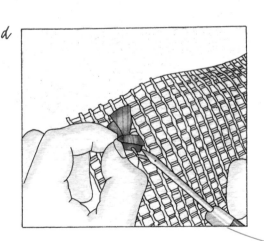

*Take your time*
*Allow yourself plenty of time to achieve this project as although the technique is fairly simple, it is very labour intensive, but well worth the effort.*

## Start the rug

*One*  Start knotting at the bottom edge of your rug canvas two holes in and two rows up (starting on the third hole and third row) and work upwards towards the top. Work left to right or right to left, whichever feels the most comfortable. Leaving two rows empty at either end will give you room to create the crochet border later.

*Two*  Carry on knotting each strip, changing colour according to your design. When working your knots, don't pull too hard. Gently pull the strips through the rug to avoid misshaping the rug canvas. After every couple of rows, using a large pair of sharp scissors, trim back the pile to approx. 4cm (1½in) in height, which creates a nice pile. This gives a welcome break to the knotting process and takes a fair bit of time in itself, so would be a very daunting task if left to the end.

Soft and welcoming, this little rug will look wonderful by the front door, or make a feature of it in front of the fireplace.

### Design Inspiration
Once you have mastered this technique you could try your hand at a rug using simple images such as daisies on the lawn using shades of whites, pinks, creams, lemons and greens.

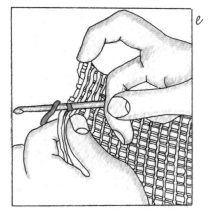

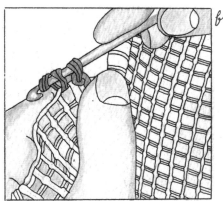

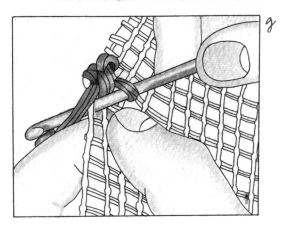

## Crochet the edge

When your rug is almost complete, with the last two rows unfinished, crochet with twine to neaten the canvas edge. Create the crocheted edge working from right to left as follows:

*One* Push the crochet hook through the first hole on the edge and pull back a loop of twine leaving a piece hanging – this can be darned into the back at the end. With the loop still in the crochet hook, catch the twine from the back of the rug, over the top of the canvas and pull it through the loop to create a stitch **(e)**.

*Two* Put the hook into the next hole and catch the twine from the back again and pull it through the hole to create your second stitch. Then, catching the twine from over the top, pull it through the two loops already on the hook, leaving you with one stitch remaining on the hook **(f)**.

*Three* Push the hook through the third hole and continue on along the rug as in step two. Try to keep the twine taut whilst working to achieve an even edge **(g)**.

Crochet in twine makes a distinctive edging, adding to the homely, rustic feel that rag rugs would have had generations ago.

## Finish the rug

*One* Tie in the twine ends and catch back with a few stitches. Finish knotting your last rows and trim back. Give the rug a quick shake and a final trim back to shorten any untidy long ends.

*Two* To back the rug, take the hessian backing, press the excess under to give the correct size, pin to the reverse of your rug and slipstitch into position. Stab stitch a few stitches through all the layers to hold in place.

# falling leaves

Summer is over and in the blink of an eye the woods and countryside are ablaze with fiery colours. When out on walks with the children, a favourite game is to catch a falling leaf for good luck, although most of the time they are far too elusive for us and flutter away, just out of reach! As the children shuffle through wind-blown leaves, we ask them to collect as many different varieties as they can find. Then it's back home again for hot chocolate whilst we examine our finds.

This attractive throw is the outcome of just such a magical day and is perfect for snuggling under as the days draw in. It is made from a beautiful cream wool crepe and the organza leaves are taken from drawings of the real thing. Each leaf is machine embroidered to create the detail of the veins, then carefully placed over the wool, moving from corner to corner as if falling from a tree.

'Every leaf speaks bliss to me
Fluttering from the autumn tree.'
EMILY BRONTË

## You will need

- 144 x 144cm (56¾ x 56¾in) cream wool crepe
- 30 x 50cm (12 x 30in) bronze, red, orange and brown organza
- Polyester threads to complement leaves
- Three skeins dusty coral tapestry wool
- Selection of leaves (five different types and sizes)
- Double-sided fusible webbing (Bondaweb)
- Chalk pencil

## Prepare

*One* Collect an assortment of leaves from different trees when you are next out on a walk. Either put them in a flower press or between sheets of absorbent paper (blotting paper or kitchen roll) under several heavy books. Leave for a couple of weeks until dry and very flat. This could be done at any time of the year. Although we went out collecting in fall, the time of year and the leaves you choose may influence your choice of colour and type of fabric for this project. For a summer throw, you might wish to use a muted green georgette and appliqué your leaves in shades of green doupion to give a devore effect.

*Two* Press the wool crepe under 1cm (⅜in) along each edge and pin. In contrasting tapestry wool, blanket stitch around the outside, catching in the 1cm (⅜in) turning.

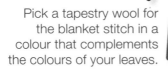

Pick a tapestry wool for the blanket stitch in a colour that complements the colours of your leaves.

## Make the leaves

*One* When the leaves have completely dried out, use them as templates and draw around them on to plain paper, detailing all the veins. You can simplify or stylize them to make it easier for yourself later on when you begin the machine embroidery. We chose five different leaf shapes including beech, oak and sycamore. Draw your leaves on to the Bondaweb and fuse on to the organza. We chose bronze, orange, red and brown organza, but you really could choose any colour.

*Two* Cut out the leaves. Lay the throw out on a clean surface or floor and start having some fun with your leaf shapes. We wanted to give the illusion of the wind blowing the leaves in a diagonal direction so that although they were all over the throw, the majority was gathered at the bottom corner. Alternatively, you could swirl them in a spiral or just intersperse them evenly over the surface.

*Three* When you are happy with your final positioning, pin the leaves down and carefully fuse them to the wool using a pressing cloth.

Let nature be your inspiration for this throw. Mark out the veins with a chalk pencil for the stitching or study your dried leaf collection and freehand embroider.

### Design Inspiration
This throw could be inspired by anything around you. Making sketches of collected beach finds while on holiday and translating them into stitch in soft, pebbly colours on a pale, sea-green wool would look stunning.

## Embroider the leaves

*One* Using your leaf templates as a guide, you can either mark out the veins with a chalk pencil or, if you feel confident enough, just refer to your templates and then freehand machine embroider the detail using a straight stitch. This will not only give a great effect but will also hold the leaves in position. Remember that as the base cloth is cream you will need to thread the bobbin with cream thread so that the stitching doesn't show on the reverse **(a)**.

*Two* After finishing each leaf, cut off all the thread ends. Remember to double back at the beginning and end of each vein so that the thread doesn't unravel. Give the throw a final press under a pressing cloth.

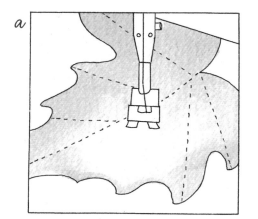
*a*

# tree of life

The apple tree is an object of great beauty that constantly changes as the seasons progress. In the spring, it displays the prettiest blossom and as summer arrives, the acid green leaves create a wonderful contrast against the bright blue sky. As fall approaches, delicious fruits weigh down the boughs and even during winter, the tree's familiar silhouette is splendid to behold. It is for these reasons that we were inspired to record its beauty in stitches with this charming cushion design.

We kept the design simple by using basic outline shapes and selecting bold colours for the leaves. The central panel has the apple tree design machine appliquéd on to it and we have used freehand machine embroidery to create sketch-like apples around the sides.

'A seed hidden in the heart of an apple is an orchard invisible'

WELSH PROVERB

## You will need

- 32 x 32cm (12½ x 12½in) natural linen for the centre panel
- 45 x 50cm (17⅝ x 20in) textured green upholstery fabric for the cushion back
- Four side panels: 39 x 9cm (15¼ x 3½in) textured green upholstery fabric
- 45 x 15cm (17⅝ x 5⅞in) textured green upholstery fabric for the front under flap
- 10cm (4in) lengths of fabrics in red, yellow, orange, blue, leaf green and emerald green for the leaves and apples
- Nine printed cotton scraps of fabrics in reds and greens for large apples on back panel
- Scrap of brown printed cotton for the tree trunk
- Ten vintage buttons: assorted sizes and colours
- Cushion pad 45cm x 45cm (17⅝ x 17⅝in)
- Double-sided fusible webbing (Bondaweb)
- Embroidery threads
- Polyester threads
- Chalk pencil
- Darning foot

You'll find the templates for this project on pages 118–119

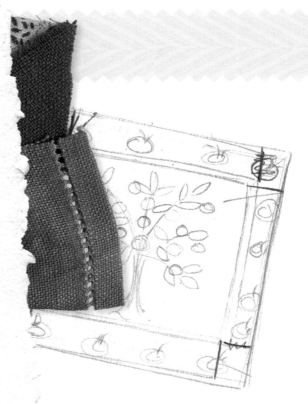

## Prepare

*One*  Draft up the pattern pieces using the dimensions as stated above. Pin the pattern pieces on to the relevant fabrics and cut out. Zigzag or overlock around each piece to neaten.

## Create the tree

*One*  To create the tree of life design, draw out thirty-nine leaves, twelve apples and the tree trunk motif on to Bondaweb. For the leaves, you will need seven in leaf green, seven in yellow, seven in orange, eight in blue, ten in emerald green and for the apples, twelve in red. Fuse and cut out. Following the plan on page 119, position and fuse the trunk. With a chalk pencil, draw out the branches and stem stitch with a dark brown embroidery thread **(a)**.

*Two*  Following the plan, position the apples and leaves to achieve an even balance of colour. When you are happy with the overall look, fuse and machine appliqué in place.

*a*

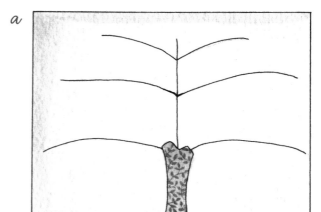

*Appliqué perfect*
If you have a good zigzag stitch on your machine, you can keep the bobbin threaded with ivory thread. If your zigzag is temperamental, you'll need to thread all your bobbins with matching thread.

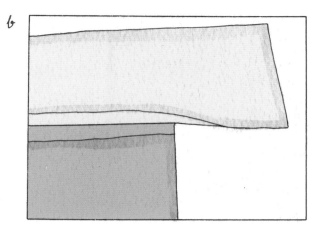

*b*

## Make the cushion front

*One*  Take the first side panel and pin to the centre panel r/s together with the left side overhanging by 8cm (3⅛in). Stitch and press the seams open **(b)**.

*Two*  Continue around the square, pinning a panel and stitching until you reach the last one. Pin and stitch up to the seam of the first panel. Stop and press the seam open, then stitch the last edge to the overhang of the first panel **(c)**.

*Three*  With the chalk pencil, draw apples directly on to the paneled border equally spaced with five to a row. If you prefer, use the template for the back piece apples on page 118 as a guide. Attach the darning foot to you machine, drop the feed dog and thread with a contrasting thread. Freehand machine embroider two or three times around the apples, then repeat with the stem and leaf. Don't be too meticulous with your stitching, you are aiming for a sketchy appearance.

*Four*  Take the front underflap facing and press in half along the length. With the r/s together, stitch the raw edges of facing to the bottom edge of the cushion front. Press and understitch the facing.

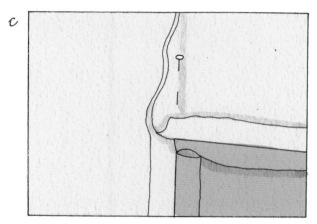

*c*

Try to achieve an even spread of colour and pack the leaves tightly together to ensure plentiful branches. Don't worry if the apples overlap the leaves; it gives a deep, three-dimensional feel.

## Add the apples and buttons

*One* To create the facing for the buttonholes, take the back cushion piece and turn the 45cm (17⅝in) bottom edge under by 1cm (⅜in), then a further 4cm (1½in) and topstitch to secure. Draw out the large apple and leaf motif using the template on page 118 on to the Bondaweb and fuse on to the nine scraps of printed red and green cotton and the remaining emerald green fabric. Position equally on to the fabric, referring to the photograph (opposite) for inspiration, fuse and machine appliqué.

*Two* Place and pin out ten vintage buttons in assorted colours and sizes on to the facing and make buttonholes. To remember where each button is positioned, run a line of sticky tape over the buttons to keep them in order **(d)**.

## Make up the cushion

*One* Make up the cushion by placing r/s together with the underflap folded over the bottom edge of the back to create a pillowcase finish. Stitch and clip the corners, then turn through and press. Sew on the buttons **(e)**.

*Two* To complete the cushion, stem stitch the grass using emerald green embroidery thread and a tiny fallen apple in red and green, referring to the photo on page 71 for positioning.

*d*

*e*

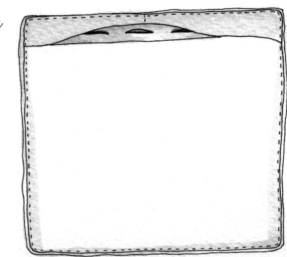

*All change*
If you prefer, all the leaves, apples and appliqués could be finished by blanket stitching or oversewing (see page 116).

The border of apples is outlined using freehand embroidery, giving a sketchy effect in contrast to the bold colours used on the Tree of Life design.

## Design Inspiration

Look at spring blossom for your inspiration and change the leaf colours to shades of soft greens. Substitute the apples with pale pink blossom that could then be used around the outside and on the back of the cushion. Instead of a fallen apple on the ground, stitch the outline of a rabbit.

By using a variety of scraps of fabric and an assorted range of vintage buttons, you can give the cushion an individual touch.

# freshly picked

This decorative hanging apple can be given an individual look by using a variety of fabric scraps left over from the Tree of Life Cushion and will look great hanging from a kitchen cupboard. Use simple beading and wirework techniques to create the stem and leaves.

## You will need

- Eight scraps of red and green cotton fabrics
- 40cm (16in) length of silver galvanized wire
- 25cm (10in) very fine jewellery wire
- Small beads in various colours
- Stuffing
- Round nosed pliers
- Wire cutters
- Red and green embroidery thread

The template for this project is on page 119

**One**  Using the template on page 119, cut out eight segments using alternate red and green cotton fabrics. With r/s together, stitch the segments together leaving a 4cm (3¼in) gap in the centre of the last seam. Clip the curves and trim excess at the top and bottom. Turn through, stuff and close the opening with a slipstitch. With the embroidery threads, herringbone stitch over each seamline.

**Two**  Sew a bead at the point where all the seams meet at the top and the bottom by stabbing the needle through the entire apple. Gently pull the two beads towards each other a little to create a slight dimple.

**Three**  For the stem and leaves, take a 40cm (16in) length of silver galvanized wire. Using round nosed pliers create a 5mm (³⁄₁₆in) loop. Next create the stem by taking the wire up by 3cm (3⅛in) and bending it back down towards the loop. Wind the wire closely around the stem up to the 1cm (³⁄₈in) mark. Take the wire out to one side to make a leaf shape and then back towards the centre and repeat on the other side. Twist both leaves to bring them close to the stem. Now wind the rest of the wire up to the top of the stem and back down where you can trim it back using wire cutters.

**Four**  Using about 25cm (10in) of a very fine jewellery wire, wind the end tightly around the top outer point of the left leaf. Pick up one small bead and take it across the bottom outer point. Secure the bead by winding the wire around it a few times. Continue back and forth across the leaf by adding two, three, then four beads, then reducing to end up a with one bead at the final point. Trim back the wire and repeat with the other leaf. Attach the stem to the top of the apple by securing through the bead. Hang the apple using a thin piece of thread.

## Baked Apples...
### ...a simple but satisfying treat!

- four large apples • A handful of raisins, currants and sultanas • Golden syrup

1. Core the apples and slit the skins around the middle.
2. Place in a dish and fill with the fruit. Drizzle a spoonful of syrup over the top.
3. Cook for around 45 minutes in a preheated oven at 180°C (350°F), Gas mark 4.
4. Serve with fresh cream or homemade custard... enjoy!

# heavenly heirloom

Creating handmade gifts for the special people in our lives gives us immense pleasure. The angel is a symbol of peace, hope and tranquility and so is a perfect choice to make as an heirloom doll to pass down through the family. Made from calico with jute twine hair, her special dress is from our collection of vintage lace and embroidered linens, applied using crazy patchwork – a technique of placing lace, trim and fabric side by side to create wonderful patterns and textures.

For the finishing touches, we have created an ornate halo, made from gold wire with tiny beaded felt stars, and no angel would be complete without a pair of divine golden wings. With a handy loop at the neck, she can be displayed at the top of your festive tree or placed above the bed of a little one as a guardian of her dreams.

'Hush! My dear, lie still and slumber,
Holy angels guard thy bed!
Heavenly blessing without number
Gently falling on thy head.'

ISAAC WATTS

## You will need

· 50cm (20in) calico or flesh-coloured cotton for the doll body
· A variety of vintage linens, tea tray cloths, laces and trims for crazy patchwork
· 30 x 45cm (12 x 17¾in) lightweight white linen or cotton for skirt base
· 25cm (9¾in) lace to cover centre back seam
· 20cm (8in) thin white velvet ribbon for the waistband
· 20cm (8in) bias binding for neck of dress
· 30 x 12cm (12 x 4¾in) good quality plain linen for the bodice
· 20 x 40cm (8 x 15¾in) decorative broderie anglaise for sleeves
· 25 x 20cm (9¾ x 8in) gold felt for wings
· 50 x 20cm (20 x 8in) gold doupion for wings
· Four 50cm (20in) lengths of twine
· Twenty-six 42cm (16½in) lengths of twine
· Knitting needle or blunt end of a fine paintbrush
· Toy stuffing
· Double-sided fusible webbing (Bondaweb)
· Embroidery threads for embellishment
· Polyester threads
· 70cm (27½in) thin gold jewellery wire for halo
· Scrap of gold felt for stars on halo
· Five tiny gold beads
· Chalk pencil

You'll find the templates for this project on page 124

## Construct the body

*One*  Scale up the patterns from page 124 and transfer on to pattern paper. Pin and cut out the pieces for the dolls body and transfer all markings and balance marks. With r/s together, pin and stitch the main body at the shoulders and then at the side seams from the balance mark. Press the seams open. With r/s together, pin and stitch the legs, arm and head pieces. Trim and clip. Turn through and press. Stuff the legs fully and stitch across the top on the s/a to enclose the ends. Stuff the arms firmly but not fully yet. Do not enclose end.

*Two*  Take the main body and insert the unstuffed head into the neck opening r/s together, matching up at the side seams. Pin and hand sew these together with a strong, small backstitch (double thread) on the s/a line. Turn through and press. Press under the s/a on the main body at the sleeve opening and the leg opening. This gives you a good edge for attaching the limb pieces later. Stuff firmly into the head and lightly into the main body.

*Three*  Insert the arms and pin, making sure to line up the side seams at the armpit and shoulder seam. Sew all the way round with a small backstitch **(a)**. Stuff well into the arms and shoulders and finish stuffing the body fully.

*Four*  Pin the centre point between the two leg openings. Insert the legs, ensuring they are the same length, and pin. Stab stitch through to secure **(b)**.

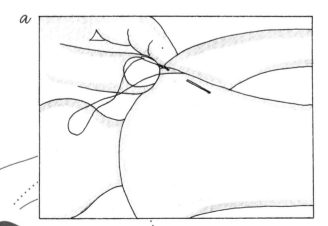

*a*

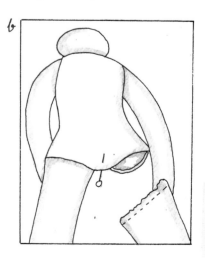

*b*

*Turn around*
A rouleaux turner is a good way to turn through the slim leg and arm pieces.

## Add the hair and face

*One* Take the four longer strands of twine. Fold in half to find the midpoint and with a double thread, attach to the front of the centre hairline, one at a time with a backstitch **(c)**. Using the 26 shorter lengths, continue working towards the back in the same way, one at a time following the centre back until all the head is covered.

*c*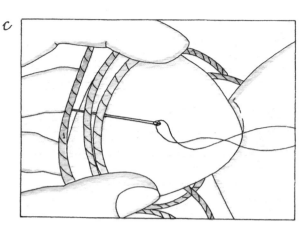

We love the texture of twine for the hair, contrasting with the delicate finery of her dress, but you could replace it with wool if you prefer.

*Two* Leaving the front four lengths loose and starting from strand five, secure at the side seams and stitch across the head **(d)**.

*Three* Take the front four lengths and twist lightly backwards towards the head. Take these around to the back and secure in a loose ponytail with a few stitches. Secure at the sides if necessary, too. Trim the hair.

*Four* Draw on your face with a fine, soft chalk pencil. Using normal sewing thread, embroider the eyes with an overstitch, the nose with two tiny French knots and the mouth with backstitch.

*d*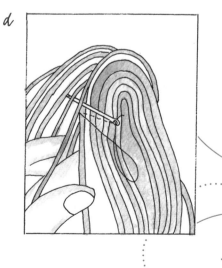

# Make the dress

*One* Cut out the skirt pattern in your soft, white linen base cloth and with r/s together, sew up the side seams but leave the back open. Press and neaten the seams. Lay your skirt flat, ready to apply the crazy patchwork.

*Two* To crazy patchwork, first cut a random shape with straight edges and as many sides as you wish –between three and five sides work well. Place in the centre of your work with r/s together and on one edge stitch with a 5mm (³⁄₁₆in) s/a **(e)**. Press the seam flat to the right side. Cut another shape as above and lay this r/s together over another edge of your central shape **(f)**. Stitch on the s/a and press over to the right side. Keep adding shapes and alternating between stitching and ironing as you work outwards **(g)**. Trim back as necessary. If you have a pretty piece of lace trim, lay this over r/s up and edge stitch into position. Have some fun, letting your fabrics lead you. If there are a few raw areas, you can embellish over these later.

*e*

*f*

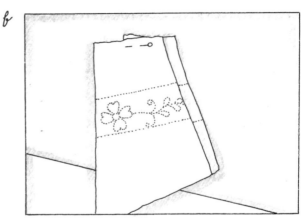

*g*

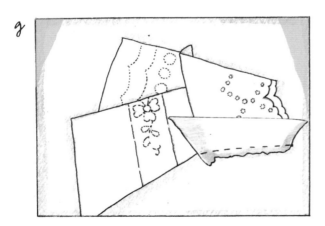

*h*

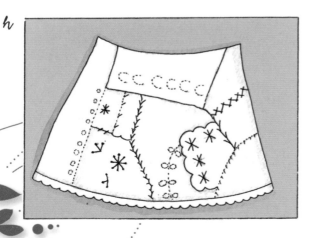

*Three* Once you have covered your base cloth you can start embellishing. Using the embroidery threads and beads that you have collected, embellish to your heart's content. Use the embroidery stitches in the stitch library (page 109) to help you. Little stars and lazy daisies give a good effect to cover plainer patches. Outlining a trim with a running stitch, feather stitch and French knots also works well. When you are happy with your completed patchwork, with r/s together, pin the two edges of the skirt together to create the centre back seam. Stitch, neaten, turn and press. Stitch on a lace trim to hide the back seam. Using a pretty trim, edge the bottom hem of the dolls skirt to finish off and embellish as desired **(h)**.

**Four** To make up the bodice, cut the main body pieces in plain fabric and with r/s together stitch side seams and shoulder seams. Neaten seams, centre back and hem edges with a tiny zigzag, press and turn. Neaten the raw neck edge by applying a bias binding facing. With r/s together, stitch your binding to the neck edge. Clip curves, turn facing to the inside of bodice and press. Slipstitch to secure. Press s/a under on the right hand back piece.

**Five** Cut out the sleeves in a pretty broderie anglaise fabric using the decorative edge as the sleeve hem. With a long stitch approx 4–5mm (⁵⁄₃₂–³⁄₁₆in) and without double backing, machine stitch a row of stitches to gather up at the sleeve head. With r/s together, sew the side seams, press and neaten. Insert the sleeve into the bodice, easing the gathers in, pin and hand stitch with a small backstitch. Neaten and turn to the right side.

**Six** With r/s together, attach the bodice to the skirt at the waist, press and neaten. Cover the join with a pretty piece of thin velvet ribbon and embroider French knots around the neck opening and embroider a heart on the front of the bodice with a tiny running stitch. Dress your doll and secure the bodice back seam with an overstitch.

## Design Inspiration

The design alternatives are endless. By changing the hairstyle and clothes you could make girl and boy dolls. Why not change the wings to a butterfly shape and add splashes of colour to transorm your angel into a pretty fairy doll?

## Sew the wings

*One* Take a piece of Bondaweb approx. 50 x 20cm (20 x 8in) and fuse on to the doupion. Peel off the paper and place the felt on to one half of the doupion (Bondaweb side up). Fold the other half of doupion over the felt and fuse. You now have a sandwich of doupion on either side with the felt in the middle. Draft up the wing pattern (page 124). Pin on to the doupion sandwich and cut out. Using the photo, right, for guidance, transfer the stitched wing detail and sew with a machine straight stitch or hand stem stitch. Neaten the edge with zigzag and finally finish with a small blanket stitch in complementary embroidery thread. Highlight the stitching with beads.

*Two* Fold a 10cm (4in) piece of velvet ribbon in half to create a hanging loop and attach with an overstitch to the centre back of the doll (approx. 3cm/1⅛in from the neck edge).

*Three* Pin the wings on to the centre back of the doll, making sure to conceal the edge of the ribbon within them. Backstitch them into position. Finally, oversew across the centre bottom of the wings to create dimension.

With her doupion wings, detailed with stitching and beads, this doll is the perfect gift for your own little angel.

## Coil the halo

*One* Take the gold wire and coil it around twice to fit the dolls head (approx. 8cm/3⅛in). Wind the rest in and out of the circle to give a wreath-like effect. Cut five tiny felt stars and sew a bead on the centre of each one. Sew at regular intervals around the halo ensuring that one is placed at the front. Attach the halo to the dolls head at either side and at the centre back.

# star struck

For a quick variation on the main project, make up a delicate hanging star from a piece of crazy patchwork mounted on to a star shape calico base. Embellish, embroider and back by fusing on to a good weight wool felt and cutting out. Hold in place at the edges with a machine zigzag and neaten with a blanket stitch. Attach a hanging loop and finish with beads or buttons at the points.

# gorgeous garland

A lovely Christmas tradition is to hang a holly wreath from the front door to welcome your visitors. We thought it would be nice to create an indoor version that could be hung from either a door or the wall and could be used year after year as part of your festive decorations. We have designed a very contemporary, stylized holly wreath using a beautiful green printed silk for the leaves and embellished it with a combination of buttons and beads.

The base of the wreath is very simple to make and you can easily vary the decoration to make a floral garland like the one we have shown on page 90. This is certain to become a firm favourite and something you look forward to putting up every year.

'Deck the halls with boughs of holly,
Fa la la la la, la la la la.'
TRADITIONAL SONG

## You will need

· 4m (154in) millinery wire
· 12 x 120cm (4¾ x 47in) approx. wadding
· 12 x 120cm (4¾ x 47in) green linen
· Wire cutters
· Small round nose pliers
· 30–40 green buttons
· Scrap of red felt
· 25 x 112cm (9¾ x 44¼in) medium-weight printed cotton or silk for leaves
· Twenty-one red, berry-like beads
· Green and red multi-purpose sewing threads
· Small quantity of toy stuffing
· 25 x 120cm (9¾ x 47in) green felt for leaves
· Masking tape
· 20cm (8in) green bias binding

You'll find the templates for this project on page 121

## Form the wire base

*One* Taking one end of the millinery wire, shape a 28cm (11in) diameter circle and fasten the end with masking tape. Continue to wind around the remaining wire, smoothing between your thumb and first finger to create a firm ring. Wrap this closely together with masking tape, which will be covered.

*Two* To create the hanging loop, cut 30cm (12in) of millinery wire with wire cutters and wind one end tightly to the wire wreath base using the pliers. Form a loop with the next 12–14cm (4¾–5½in) of wire. Fasten back to the wreath base with a couple of turns. Then pull the loop a little closer together and twist the remaining wire around to hold secure **(a)**. Wrap a small strip of bias binding carefully around the loop and secure with a couple of stitches.

*Three* Cut three widths of wadding 4cm (1½in) wide and wind evenly around the wreath base, joining on more as necessary with a couple of stitches. Secure at the end **(b)**.

*a*

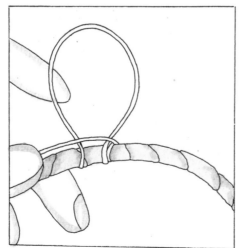

*b*

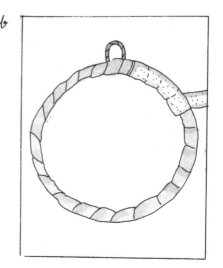

*Four* Cut the green linen into three pieces, each 4 x 120cm (1½ x 47in), making sure it is cut on the straight grain, and join together along the short edges. Machine topstitch 2mm (³⁄₃₂in) from the left-hand edge along the entire strip. Fray the edge back just shy of the stitch line. Starting at the loop, attach the strip to the wadding with a couple of stitches and then start to wind around the wreath base in a clockwise direction, covering the raw edge and leaving the frayed edge visible **(c)**.

 *c*

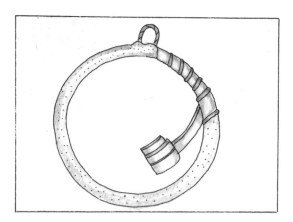

Pick and mix your green buttons to add variety to the design.

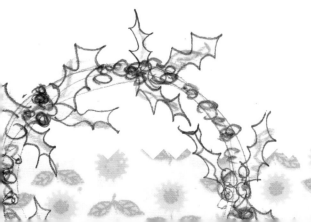

## Make the holly leaves

*One* Cut out 21 leaf shapes and pin w/s together on to your felt backing. Stitch just inside the edge of each leaf, leaving a small opening for the stuffing. Cut out and lightly stuff. Machine stitch the gap closed. Zigzag over the raw edges to neaten. Highlight the central vein with a backstitch in green embroidery thread.

*Two* Take three leaves and sew together with a few stab stitches. Cut out 21 red felt circles between 1cm (³⁄₈in) and 2cm (¾in) diameter for the berries. Attach to the trio of leaves with a cross-stitch and finish with a red ceramic bead **(d)**. Position these arrangements in clusters around the main wreath. Pin and stitch by hand. To complete your wreath, sew green buttons between the holly leaves.

 *d*

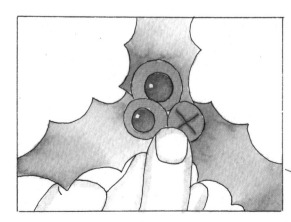

# say it with flowers

Why wait until Christmas to hang up a decorative wreath? This floral design is made in the same way as the holly garland, but uses a lilac silk for the petals and is embellished with exquisite crystal beads and treasured buttons.

### Design Inspiration
Taking the holidays as inspiration, make a garland for each festive occasion – chicks and colourful eggs for Easter, hearts for Valentine's or bats and pumpkins for Halloween.

## You will need

- 30 x 40cm (12 x 15¾in) lilac doupion for the 24 petals
- 30 x 40cm (12 x 15¾in) iron-on interfacing
- Approx. 12 x 120cm (4¾ x 47in) wadding
- 5 x 240cm (2 x 94½in) champagne silk satin
- 20cm (8in) champagne satin bias binding
- 12 x 60cm (4¾ x 23½in) pale green silk organza for the leaves
- Double-sided fusible webbing (Bondaweb)
- 4m (154in) millinery wire
- Wire cutters
- Small round nosed pliers
- 30–40 glass and mother-of-pearl buttons
- Six crystal and glass beads
- Chalk pencil
- Masking tape

You'll find the templates for this project on page 121

**One** Make up the wire garland base and add wadding following the instructions for the holly garland (page 88). Cut a strip of satin 5cm x 240cm (2 x 94½in) long. Press one long edge over 1cm (⅜in) to the w/s. Gently wind around your wreath base as for the holly garland but covering the raw edge. Secure the ends together with a tiny overstitch.

**Two** Fuse the interfacing on to the wrong side of the lilac doupion. Using a chalk pencil, draw around the petal template and mark out 24 petals on to the interfacing. Machine straight stitch the petals just inside your chalk line. Add some vein details with a machine topstitch, double backing at the start and finish of each stitch line **(a)**.

**Three** Cut out the petals on the chalk line. Fold in half with r/s together and sew a tiny dart to curve the petal. With r/s together, sew pairs of petals together with a small seam 2.5mm (⅛in) from the dart end. Lay two pairs of petals together and join at the centre with a few stitches. Repeat with the remaining pairs.

**Four** Draw out 12 Bondaweb leaves using the template and fuse on to the back of the organza. Cut out and peel off the backing. Place the leaves, Bondaweb side down, on to another piece of organza and fuse under a pressing cloth. Stitch the leaves 1mm (¹⁄₂₀in) inside the outline and carefully cut out **(b)**.

**Five** Position the flowers evenly around the garland and pin on two leaves underneath each flower. Catch the leaves down first with a few small stitches and attach the flowers in the same way over the top. Neaten and finish at the centre with a glass bead. To complete your garland, sew on glass and mother-of-pearl buttons between the flowers.

*b*

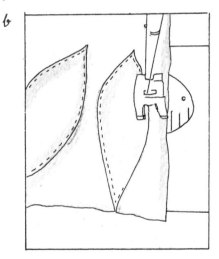

*a*

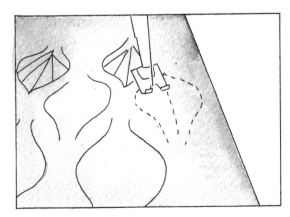

### The silk route

Satin and silky fabrics make a luxurious base for your wreaths but take extra care when winding it around your wadded base. Avoid unsightly puckers by allowing the fabric to curve gently and find its own natural position rather than pulling it taught.

# filled with memories

The end of the year is a time when we reminisce about the previous year and what it has meant to us. We decided that a memory book would be a great place to put these cherished recollections, collected photos, drawings, jottings, cuttings and recipes.

The cover design is inspired by the cycle of the year and the motifs are taken from previous projects in the book and represent the seasons of our sewing year. Pale green silk fabric is appliquéd and hand embroidered with our sweet song thrush to represent spring, pretty flowers recall summer, falling leaves settle at the bottom corner, leading the eye around to the glossy green and red of the winter holly.

The book construction is simple and understated using good quality papers and is finished with a Japanese binding technique, allowing the decorative cover to take centre stage.

'Take care of all your memories.
For you cannot relive them.'
BOB DYLAN
(American folksinger)

## You will need

- Graph or squared paper
- A1 sheet mounting card
- 12 sheets of watercolour paper (300g)
  31cm wide x 27cm tall (31¼ x 10½in)
- A1 sheet contrast paper (150g) for lining inside covers
  and binding edges
- 50cm x 120cm (20in x 47in) pale green silk doupion for
  front and back cover
- 2m (78½in) leather twine 2mm (¹⁄₁₀in) thick
- Scraps of fabric for appliqué in silk doupion and linen:
  - bright green for holly
  - lime green for leaves
  - browns for bird and branch
  - burnt oranges, golds and reds for autumn leaves
  - pale pink for blossom
  - red for berries
  - aubergine for the numbers.
- Embroidery silks in complementary colours
- Chalk pencil
- Bone folder
- Cutting mat, metal ruler, set square and craft knife
- Two long elastic bands
- Four large bulldog/fold back office clips
- Fabric adhesive spray
- PVA white glue
- Electric drill with 4mm wood drill bit

You'll find the templates for this project on page 125
and embroidery stitches on page 109.

## Prepare

**One** Scale up the design on page 125 on to graph paper, adding your desired year to the centre using the number guide. Reverse the templates, draw on to Bondaweb, fuse to your chosen fabrics and cut out. Take the silk doupion and cut out the front cover 40 x 40cm (15¾ x 15¾in) and mark out a 28cm (11in) square with tacking stitch. Referring to the design, lay out the appliqué shapes within this square and fuse into position ensuring that all of the design finishes at least 5mm (³⁄₁₆in) inside the edges.

**Two** Using a chalk pencil, transfer all details to be embroidered on to the fused shapes.

## Embroider the cover

**One** Using matching embroidery threads, overstitch all the way around the bird, branch and leaves. In a slightly darker thread, backstitch the tail and wing details. Stitch little v shapes along the breast, embroider a bullion stitch for the eye and a long stitch for the beak. For the feet, make a long stitch and then sew a diagonal stitch either side to create the three claws. Add detail to the leaves with a backstitch for the midrib and two v stitches through the middle as veins. For the feathers, split an embroidery thread to a single strand and stemstitch down the centre. Complete with diagonal overstitches either side.

**Two** Outline the flowers with a chain stitch in a matching embroidery thread. Create the stamens with a collection of bullion stitches in pale yellow thread. Overstitch around the leaves then add detail as before. Embroider lazy daisies in several coordinating coloured threads into the corner and add stamen detail with French knots.

**Three** Overstitch around each autumn leaf in matching embroidery thread. Backstitch all vein details. Backstitch around the apples in red and green embroidery threads.

**Four** Overstitch around the holly leaves and the stem in matching threads. Carefully backstitch around the edge of berries. Add the leaf detail as before. For the snowflakes, create a star shape by stitching a large cross with a smaller cross sewn on top. Then, oversew little stitches over the star shape to finish.

**Five** For the date, overstitch around the numbers in a matching embroidery thread. If you prefer, you could stitch a name or phrase here.

**Six** When the embroidery is complete, give it a final press and cut back the silk to (width x height) 31.5 x 32cm (12⅜ x 12⅝in). This includes a s/a of 2cm (¾in) around the top, bottom and right side edges and a s/a of 1.5cm (⅝in) at the left (binding edge). Remove the tacking stitches.

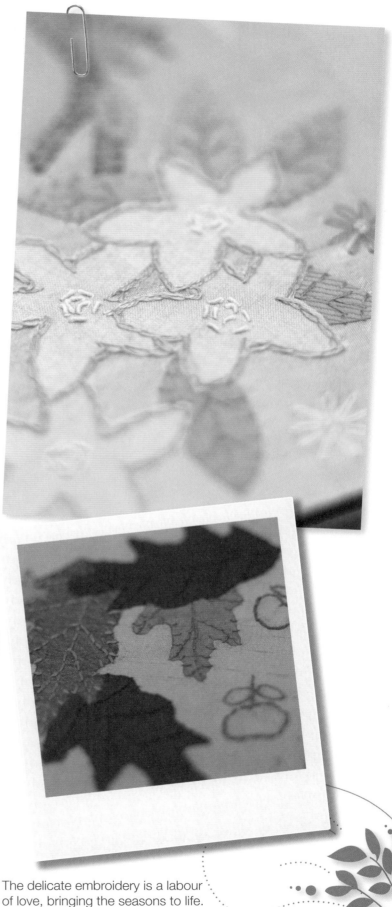

The delicate embroidery is a labour of love, bringing the seasons to life.

## Cut the card and paper

*One* Cut out the mounting card (width x height): back cover 31.8 x 28cm (12½ x 11in); front cover (in two parts) 2 x 28cm (¾in x 11in) and 29.5 x 28cm (11⅝ x 11in).

*Two* From the contrast paper, cut two pieces 31 x 5.3cm (12³⁄₁₆ x 2⅛in) for the binding edge. Label A. Cut two pieces 4.5 x 27.8cm (1¾ x 11in) for inside binding edge lining. Label B. Cut one piece 29 x 27.5cm (11⅜ x 10¾in) for front cover inside lining. Label C. Cut one piece 30.5 x 27.5cm (12 x 10¾in) for back cover inside lining. Label D. Cut a minimum of 12 pages in watercolour paper 31x 27cm (12³⁄₁₆ x 10½in).

## Assemble the front cover

*One* Apply a fine covering of spray mount to the front cover mounting card. Place the embroidered silk with r/s up over the top of the card following instructions for s/as given in step six, page 95. Starting at the centre smooth out, removing creases. Cut across the corners leaving a 5mm (³⁄₁₆in) s/a. Bring the top and bottom s/as over the card to the back and glue into position, smoothing out as you go. Dab a bit of glue on your corner points and with your finger nail, tuck in the raw edge of the corner. Bring the right side s/a over to the back of the card and glue into position **(a)**. The left hand edge will be covered by the contrast binding paper and so is not turned under like the other edges.

*Two* Now, line the front cover with the inside lining paper (C). Spread the inside of the front cover evenly with PVA glue. Carefully place the lining paper over this and smooth out all bumps **(b)**. Leave to dry.

*Spread it around*
Use a spreader or scrap of mounting card to evenly distribute the PVA glue on to the contrast paper.

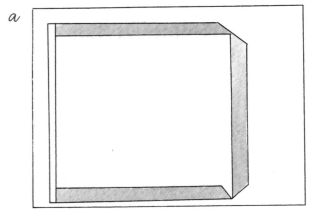

a

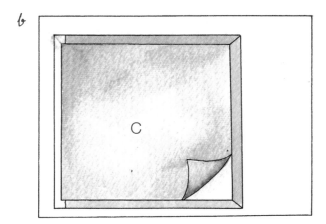

b

C

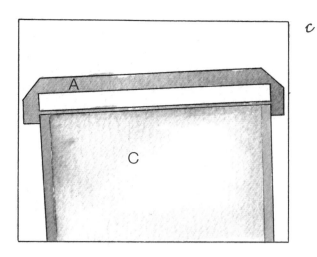

c

d

## Add the bound edge

*One*  Measure in 1.5cm (⅝in) along the left hand edge of the front cover and draw a chalk line. This line is where the bound edge contrast paper (A) will start. Take this paper and evenly spread PVA glue to the inside. Line one edge up with the chalk line and, with even amounts overlapping at top and bottom, smooth down to secure. Turn over to the w/s and lay the narrow piece of mounting card on to the contrast paper leaving a 3mm (⅛in) gap. Cut the corners back as illustrated, just 2.5mm (¹⁄₁₆in) away from the corner point **(c)**.

*Two*  On the w/s, fold over the excess paper at the top and bottom. With a fingernail, fold in the tiny corner point and then fold in the remaining paper. Smooth down to ensure it is all secured with the glue. When this is dry, turn back to the r/s and with a bone folder or the back of your fingernail, gently create a crease line within the gap in the card **(d)**. Do not cut through the paper.

*Three*  Turn to w/s again and attach a pre-glued contrast paper lining (B). Smooth as before. Add the crease from the inside in the same way as before and re-crease both sides until there is a bend at this point. This will allow the book to open easily.

## Assemble the back cover

*One*  Cut out 32 x 32cm (12⅝ x 12⅝in) green silk for the back cover. Press well and then spray mount on to the card in the same way as for the front cover. Smooth out all creases. Clip corners as before and fold over edges to the inside, securing with glue. Mark a line 4cm (1½in) in from the left hand edge in tailors chalk. Position the contrast paper (A) on to this line, glue into place and clip corners as before. Finish inside linings as for front cover.

### Cutting edge
To accurately measure and cut paper or card, always use a set square, a metal ruler, a cutting mat with grid and a sharp craft knife. Once you have marked up your cutting line and with even pressure, gently score with the craft knife, repeating until the paper/card is cut.

Once complete, you can take great pleasure in adding your collected bits and pieces as a lovely way to preserve the passing of the year.

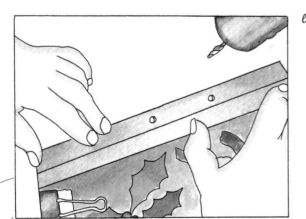

*e*

## Assemble the book

*One* Cut as many sheets of watercolour paper as you wish (we have used 12). Pile up, ensuring that all edges are straight. Keep the stack tightly together with a couple of long elastic bands around the pages. Make a sandwich with the back cover, the pages stack and the front cover and hold in place with bulldog clips. A small piece of cloth placed underneath these will protect the cover.

*Two* Mark out five hole positions at even intervals along the bound edge 1.5cm (⅝in) in and 1.5cm (⅝in) from each end. Place on an off-cut of wood on a secure workbench or table. Get someone to help you by holding the book so it doesn't move. Drill the holes using the 4mm wood drill bit **(e)**. Smooth around the holes with the back of a fingernail.

## Binding

**One** Keeping the book clamped together with the clips, create the Japanese binding finish. Take the leather cord and tape one end tightly with some clear sticky tape about 3cm (1⅛in) up to make threading easier. If you are using ribbon you will need to thread this into a needle.

**Two** With the book cover facing up, start at the second hole in from the left. Pass the cord from the top side down through the hole, leaving an end of about 25cm (9¾in). Bring the cord up around the spine and pass down through the hole again. It will now be on the underside. Bring it up through the next hole to the right, then around the spine and up again through the same hole. Continue with the next hole to the right, working around the spine in the same way, and repeat with the last hole. The cord should now be on the topside of the last hole. Bring the cord around the tail end of the spine and up through the bottom hole again. The cord can now travel back towards the left in an up and down pattern (without going around the spine) until you reach the first hole on the far left. Bring this around the spine and up again through the hole and repeat the tail end process as on the other end. Your cord will now be to the top side of the first hole. Bring it over to join your starting point, tuck it under and tie a knot **(f)**.

**Three** Tie a decorative bow to finish and trim ends back as necessary.

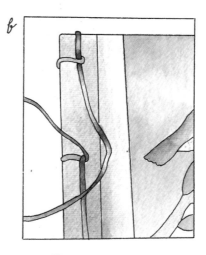

*f*

### Design Inspiration

There are so many design possibilities for this book. You could use images of food and kitchen utensils for a recipe book or flowers, vegetables and garden tools for a gardening journal. It could be used as a very special diary or even as a photograph album to store your favourite photos.

The simple binding with leather cord will keep your book intact for many years to come.

# inspiration and design

Here we just want say a few words about the inspiration and design processes with reference to the surface decoration of your projects.

There's that old saying that nothing is completely original. We draw influences from things around us all the time, sometimes intentionally and at other times without realizing it. It may be that we draw inspiration from nature, colour themes or bits and pieces that we have collected. The knack is to take these things and then add your own twist or idea.

So ... where to start? An inspiration book or pin board is a great way of collecting together all of your ideas. Within this you might have little sketches, scraps of fabrics, paint samples, magazine cuttings, postcards or poems and quotes. If you have a camera, get into the habit of carrying it around with you and capturing the things that interest you to use at a later date. Things that inspire you might be as diverse as the texture of the bark on a tree to your coffee mug and morning treat. You might love the sea and shoreline with its sailing boats, esplanades and beach huts. Inspirations from wildlife and nature are endless too. We have used flowers, fruit, birds, leaves and creepy crawlies in some of the projects within this book.

As well as looking for beautiful imagery and colours, you may also be inspired by the purpose of an object, for example, to create an heirloom gift, a throw to keep you warm or a game to keep the kids amused. We have given you a flavour of our inspirations within the mood board material at the start of each project.

## Design

Once you have gathered your inspiration, the next step is to translate these into a design. Sketches need not be finished; they help to put down your initial ideas on to paper and work through your thought processes. For example, you may produce a series of sketches of a bird and as your ideas evolve, you can pick the elements of each sketch that you like best and use these to work towards a finished design. If you don't feel confident about drawing, photocopy a photo or image from a magazine or book and trace around it to give you the outline shape. A photocopier is also a useful tool in designing as you can use it to enlarge or reduce the size of your image.

As the design progresses, add some colour. This could be as simple as adding a wash in paint or sketching in coloured pencils and this will start to get you thinking about fabrics or threads that you may

wish to use later on. Mixing pattern and colour is a very personal choice. Experiment with your fabrics to arrive at a result that pleases you. With practise this will become easier. If you feel unsure about choosing colours, it may be worth investing in an artist's colour wheel, which will give you guidance as to which colours complement each other.

Patterns, plaids and plain fabrics can be mixed together, but try to have a common colour link between each of them. Generally, smaller patterns work more successfully with smaller areas of appliqué, reserving larger prints for bigger sections.

A number of the projects within the book use appliqué and we suggest that when you design your own motifs, you keep the shapes simple and limit the amount of fabrics and colours you use. Break down the design into blocks of colour and add finer details with stitch.

# fabric

We have always had a real passion for collecting interesting fabrics and in particular, find the concept of recycling exciting.

Re-purposing and being thrifty really are more essential than ever now and through saving clothing, furnishings and old fabrics and keeping your eye out for an interesting piece of cloth at a thrift shop or market, you too can quickly build up a wide selection of fabrics to use in all your sewing projects. Of course, its great fun too!

Recycled fabrics have a lovely soft quality to them that comes with lots of washing and you are not limited to fabrics that are currently available or in this season's colours. You may soon have a selection of checks, floral and retro prints, large furnishing designs, stripes and polka dots in a huge range of colours. Another advantage is that you can buy a floral print blouse in a charity shop for a lot less than a metre of fabric, and it's unlikely that anyone else will have exactly the same print in their collection.

Of course, we also buy fabric lengths but tend to choose plain good quality cloths that are more difficult to source. Increasingly, we are trying to use base cloths that come from sustainable sources, such as the lovely cotton percale that we have used in the bed linen project and the cotton/hemp canvas used in the nest apron. But just like everyone else, if there is a lovely new fabric in a gorgeous print we always feel compelled to buy it!

With old and new fabric alike, if the washing instructions allow, pre-wash to reduce the chance of shrinkage and to get rid of any finish. Once dry, press and fold. With garments, remove sleeves and collars and cut along the seams, opening out fabric into flat manageable pieces. Unpick zips and buttons and save in jars for future projects.

So, check through your old clothing and furnishings, take a trip to the local thrift shops or flea markets and start collecting. You'll be amazed at what you can find!

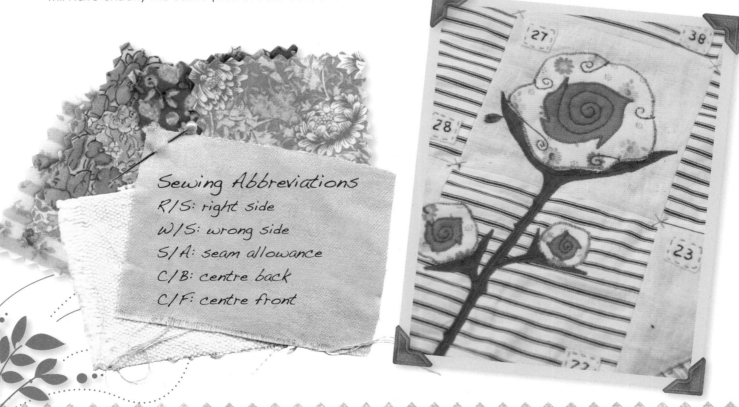

Sewing Abbreviations

R/S: right side

W/S: wrong side

S/A: seam allowance

C/B: centre back

C/F: centre front

27   38

28

23

Here is a guide to the fabrics we most often use and suggestions as to where you can salvage them from.

### Cotton

Pretty Tana Lawns, printed cottons, ginghams and checks can be sourced from shirts, blouses and dresses. Jeans and work shirts are great for the heavier weight cottons such as corduroys, denims and canvas. Cotton jersey T-shirts come in a multitude of colours. Cotton velvet can be sourced from evening dresses or soft furnishings. Printed bed linens, particularly vintage ones, are great for large-scale appliqué and linings, but check them over carefully and avoid areas of wear and tear.

### Linen

Fine linen has a lovely quality that is particularly nice to use with heirloom projects. Sources are embroidered table linen, anti-Macassars, sheets, dresses and fabric lengths.

### Wool

Vintage wool blankets are increasingly difficult to find, but persevere as they have a wonderful quality and are a great base cloth for many different applications. Knitted 100 per cent wool sweaters and cardigans can be boil washed resulting in lovely felted cloth. Other good sources can be found in suits, skirts, coats and scarves, but for a special project it is always worth investing in some top quality new cloth.

### Silk

Evening wear, ballgowns or bridesmaids' dresses are often made in silk. Have a look in your local thrift shop as outdated garments are often donated for resale and contain a tremendous amount of fabric. We have discovered many colours of silk doupion and crêpe satin in this way. You can also source lighter weight silks such as habutai and crêpe de chine from skirt linings and blouses.

# tool kit

Here are the materials and equipment required for the projects in this book.

## Sewing machine
This should be able to do straight stitch, zigzag and buttonholes. Additional foot attachments are a darning foot and walking foot.

## Machine needles
• Size 70 (9) for silks and fine cottons.
• Size 90 (14) for denims, canvas and heavy-weight linens.

## Hand-sewing needles
Straw needles are long, strong and fine so will stitch through canvas or denim but are fine enough to bead and embroider with.

## Pins
• General dressmakers' pins with glass heads or quilting pins.
• Extra-fine bridal pins for delicate fabrics.
• Safety pins for turning through channels.

## For drafting patterns
• Graph or squared paper is indispensable.
• Paper and card to make templates. You can recycle printed material or old cereal packets.
• Tape measure.
• Ruler – ideally a metal ruler giving both metric and imperial measurements.
• Set square.
• HB pencil, marker pen and sticky tape.

## Cutting tools
• Dressmaking shears (only use for fabric).
• General-purpose scissors for cutting out patterns, paper, twine and for general use.
• Embroidery scissors for fine work.
• Rotary cutter for cutting out straight lines.
• Quilters ruler to use with rotary cutter.
• Self-healing cutting mat with a cutting grid.

## Sewing threads
General-purpose polyester sewing thread.

## Embroidery threads (and hoop)
Widely available in a good range of colours, we usually split into two threads.

## Marking tools
• Chalk pencils are great for marking out stitching lines for embroidery.
• Embroidery transfer pencil.

## Double-sided fusible webbing
Available as Bondaweb (or Heat n Bond), this is a

double-sided iron-on fabric adhesive that comes on peel-off paper backing and is useful for appliqué.

## Fusible Interfacing
Use it for adding body to flimsy fabrics or for creating greater strength on straps.

## Fabric spray adhesive
Fabric spray adhesive such as Odif temporarily places a fabric, enabling you to move it around.

## Stuffing
Toy stuffing is ideal for these projects. Ensure that it carries a fire safety kite mark.

## Stitch and Tear
A useful product for creating embroidered text or detail on a project.

## Pressing equipment
• Iron for pressing and finishing.
• A pressing cloth (a square of muslin) is essential.

# basic techniques

Most of the techniques we have used for the projects are very straightforward and can be picked up quickly by a beginner. Have a practise to build up confidence before embarking on the real thing.

## Drafting a pattern and scaling up templates

The patterns and motifs in this book can be found on pages 110–125 and some will need to be scaled up on a photocopier. Your local library or printers can help with this. We have given the percentage that they need to be enlarged by. On some projects we have given accurate measurements for the fabric requirements in the You Will Need list and step instructions, therefore pattern pieces are not included. Patterns and templates can also be scaled up on to graph or squared paper, referring to the measurements with the patterns. Include all balance marks, grainlines and placement lines.

## Reversing a design

Take your drawn out design or template to a large window and, holding it up to the light, draw the outline of your shapes on to the back of your paper to reverse the design.

## Using Bondaweb

Draw the motif on to the paper backing in pencil, remembering that if the design has an obvious direction it has to be drawn in reverse. Cut roughly around the shape, leaving a margin of about 5mm (¼in) outside the pencil line. With a medium-hot iron (no steam) fuse the Bondaweb, paper side up, on to the w/s of your fabric. Cut out the motif and peel off the backing paper. Place the motif, glue side down, on to the fabric and fuse. To protect your iron always use a pressing cloth.

## Using Stitch and Tear

With a pencil, draw your design on to the Stitch and Tear, pin in position, embroider on top of the pencil line and, once complete, tear away the paper to leave the finished design.

## Transferring markings

Markings are used to illustrate the position of decorative finishes and pockets. They can be translated on to the fabric with tailors chalk or with a tacking stitch. To transfer a design for embroidery, use an embroidery transfer pencil. Draw or trace your motif on to a piece of tracing paper in a fine line, reverse the paper on to fabric and press with a warm iron for a few seconds.

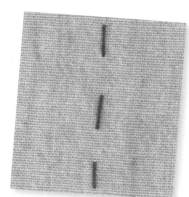

## Tacking

Tacking (basting) stitch is a longer, temporary running stitch used to hold fabric pieces together while making up. It can also be used to mark positioning lines. It can be removed once the permanent stitching is completed.

## Pinning

When pinning your pattern on to your fabric, pin the straight grain first (otherwise you may encounter problems while sewing up as the fabric will have too much ease). Then, pin around the pattern piece, diagonally at the corners and vertical to the pattern edge.

## Cutting

Ensure that your dressmaking scissors or rotary cutter is sharp. To cut accurately, position your fabric to the left of your shears (or to the right if you are left-handed), take your time and follow the edge of the pattern line, taking confident long strokes for straight edges and shorter strokes for curved areas. A rotary cutter, ruler and cutting mat are very useful for cutting out patchwork pieces and patterns with straight lines.

## Pressing

Pressing is an essential process for any sewing project and should be done at each stage of the making up. Unlike ironing, when the iron glides over the fabric surface, pressing is when the iron is pressed lightly down on to the fabric, lifted and moved to the next area. Pins and tacking stitches should be removed before pressing and you should always use a pressing cloth (preferably muslin) so that you do not mark the fabric. Steam helps when pressing thick or crease-prone fabrics.

## Clipping

Clipping (slits cut into the s/a) reduces bulk and helps a seam to curve or a corner to reach a tight point. Hold the scissor points just short of the seam line to avoid cutting the stitches. Trim an outward corner across the point.

## Appliqué

This is the technique of applying fabric shapes to a background fabric to create surface decoration. Most projects in this book are machine appliquéd using Bondaweb to apply the design (see above). For machine appliqué, with a zigzag stitch set at 2mm width (¹⁄₁₀in) and 0.5mm–1mm length (¹⁄₄₀in–¹⁄₂₀in), zigzag (also called satin stitch) very carefully around the outside edge of the motif to secure. To turn a corner, leaving the needle down into the work, lift the foot and turn. Drop the foot and continue.

## Freehand machine embroidery

This is an effective embellishment that requires a little practise to get good results. Attach your darning foot to your sewing machine and lower the feed dog. Set the stitch length to zero and machine speed to slow if you have this facility. If you are embroidering a definite design, mark it out in chalk or a transfer marker on to the fabric first. Placing your fabric in an embroidery hoop can help to keep it taut. When you start stitching, hold the fabric loosely and gently guide it to create the design. Too much pressure will make the embroidery spiky or jagged. The darning foot enables you to see where you are stitching.

## Buttons and buttonholes

Many modern sewing machines have a foot attachment that works out the size of the buttonhole for you. However, older models usually have built-in buttonhole stitch and a special foot that comes with the machine. Check your manual for instructions on how to create buttonholes. It is important to mark out the positioning (and if necessary the length marks) before sewing. When you have completed your buttonhole, take a sharp pair of embroidery scissors and cut down the centre line between the stitching.

## Beading

For tiny beads apply each one individually. Using either a beading needle or very fine straw needle, thread a length of multi-purpose sewing thread in a matching colour. Starting from the back, bring the needle through to the right side of the fabric, pick up a bead and slip it on to the needle and thread. Make a backstitch through the fabric (as close to the bead as possible) to hold in position and bring the needle out where you want the next bead.

# stitch library

The projects in this book involve machine-sewing, hand-sewing and embroidery. Here are instructions for all those stitches we have used.

## Standard machine-sewing stitches

**1. Straight stitch:** all sewing machines will sew straight stitch and it is the machine stitch that you will most commonly use. It is used in this book for sewing seams, topstitching and understitching. Unless otherwise stated, we would recommend that you set your stitch length to 2.5mm (⅛in). This gives a tidy, even stitch.

**2. Zigzag:** a versatile stitch used extensively in this book to neaten seams and edges. We also use it as a decorative edge and to hold appliqué motifs in position. To neaten seams, we suggest setting your zigzag to 2mm (1/10in) width and 2mm (1/10in) length. For using on appliqué, we suggest setting your zigzag to 2mm (1/10in) width and between 0.5mm and 1mm (1/40 –1/20in) length.

**3. Topstitching:** a straight stitch set at about 3mm (3/16in) length. It can be both decorative and functional while holding the seam firmly in place. We use it mainly on straps, pockets and waistbands. Place the machine foot to the edge of the seam and use this as a guide to keep the stitching following a straight line.

**4. Understitching:** used to keep facings and linings from rolling and becoming visible from the front. Trim back s/as to about 3mm (3/16in) and press to the side where the understitching is to be applied. Working from the right side, using a straight stitch, sew close to the pressed seam (approx. 2mm/1/10in). The facing/lining can then be turned under, pressed and will lie flat.

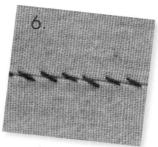

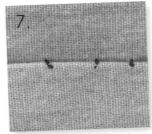

## Standard hand-sewing stitches

**5. Running stitch:** a short, even stitch that can be used for tacking, gathering and as a quilting stitch. Work from right to left, taking the needle in and out of the fabric and pulling the thread through. Keep your stitches small and space them evenly.

**6. Oversewing:** used to sew a fine seam. We use it mainly to sew up the gap after turning a project through. Make sure that the seam is turned in and, ensuring that the two folds are level and working from the right, make small even stitches over the seam at regular intervals. Oversewing can also be used as a decorative embroidery stitch.

**7. Slipstitch:** used to hem and to close gaps in seams. Work from right to left, picking up a tiny piece of the fabric from one seam edge with the needle. Insert the needle into the other seam fold and move the needle along the fold 3mm (3/16in). Push the needle out into the seam edge and repeat.

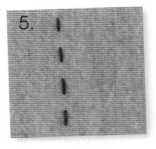

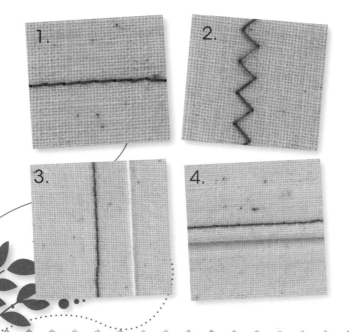

# Embroidery stitches

We generally split a cut length down into two threads, which means that one skein can last a very long time!

**1. Blanket stitch:** working left to right, secure the thread and bring it out below the edge. Insert the needle through the fabric (about 4mm (³⁄₁₆in) across and 4mm (³⁄₁₆in) up) and bring out at the edge, keeping the thread from the previous stitch under the point of the needle. Pull the thread tight to form the stitch over the edge.

**2. Stem stitch:** work from left to right along the design, taking small stitches. The needle and thread should always come out on the left side of the previous stitch.

**3. Backstitch:** insert the needle on to the design. Take a backward stitch and then bring the needle up a little way ahead of the first stitch. Insert the needle into the point where the first stitch began.

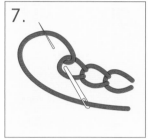

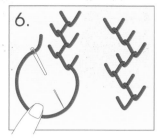

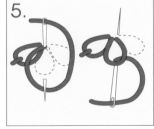

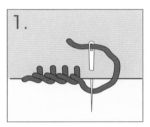

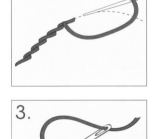

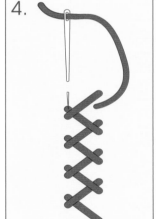

**5. Lazy daisy:** work in the same way as chain stitch, but fasten each loop at the foot with a small stitch. Group to create petals.

**6. Feather stitch:** bring the needle out at the top centre. Holding the thread down with your thumb, insert the needle to the right on the same level and take a small stitch to the centre, keeping the thread under the needle point. Inserting the needle a little to the left on the same level, take a small stitch to the centre. Repeat these two stitches, alternating between left and right.

**7. Chain stitch:** bring the thread out and hold down with the left thumb. Insert the needle where it last emerged and bring the point out a little way in front. Pull through, keeping the thread under the needle point to form the looped stitch.

**8. Bullion stitch:** insert the needle the appropriate distance from the original point, bring it back up through the first point, keep the needle in the material and twist the thread evenly around the needle the required number of times. Tighten the coil by pulling the thread and insert the needle into the end of the knot.

**4. Herringbone stitch:** bring the needle up on the lower line at the left side. Insert on the upper line to the right and with the thread below the needle, take a small stitch to the left. Then, insert the needle on to the lower line to the right with the thread above the needle and take another small stitch to the left. Continue to the end.

**9. French knots:** bring the thread to the front and hold it down with the left finger and thumb. Twist the thread around the needle twice. Insert the needle close to where the thread emerged and draw the thread tightly through, creating a neat knot on the surface.

# patterns & templates

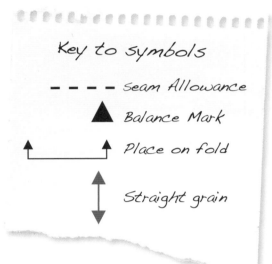

Key to symbols

- – – – – Seam Allowance
▲ Balance Mark
↑—↑ Place on fold
↕ Straight grain

## Getting Organized, pages 8–13

Wall planner design layout

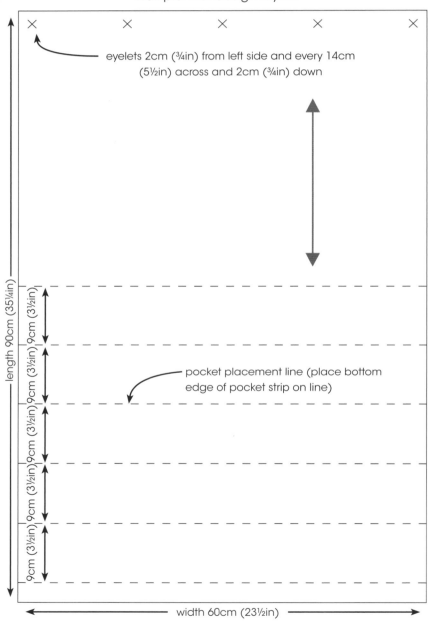

eyelets 2cm (¾in) from left side and every 14cm (5½in) across and 2cm (¾in) down

pocket placement line (place bottom edge of pocket strip on line)

length 90cm (35¼in)

9cm (3½in) 9cm (3½in) 9cm (3½in) 9cm (3½in) 9cm (3½in) 9cm (3½in)

width 60cm (23½in)

## Embroidery motifs

January  February  March

April  May  June

July  August  September

October  November  December

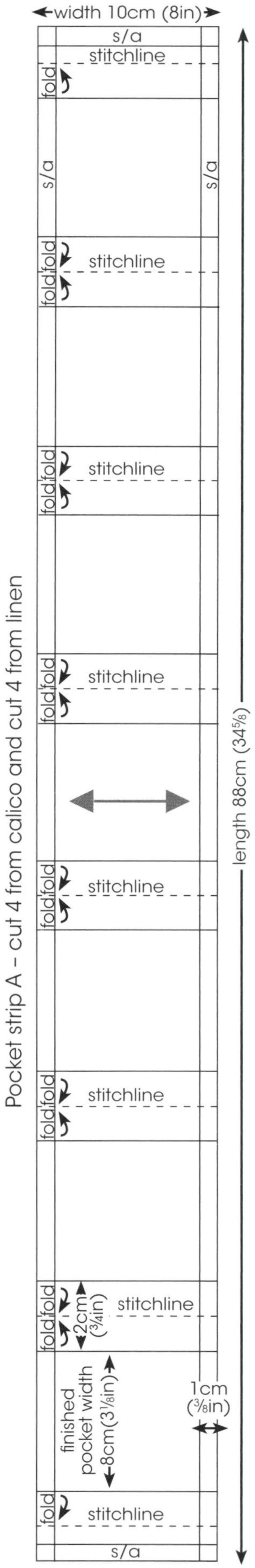

Patchwork layout design

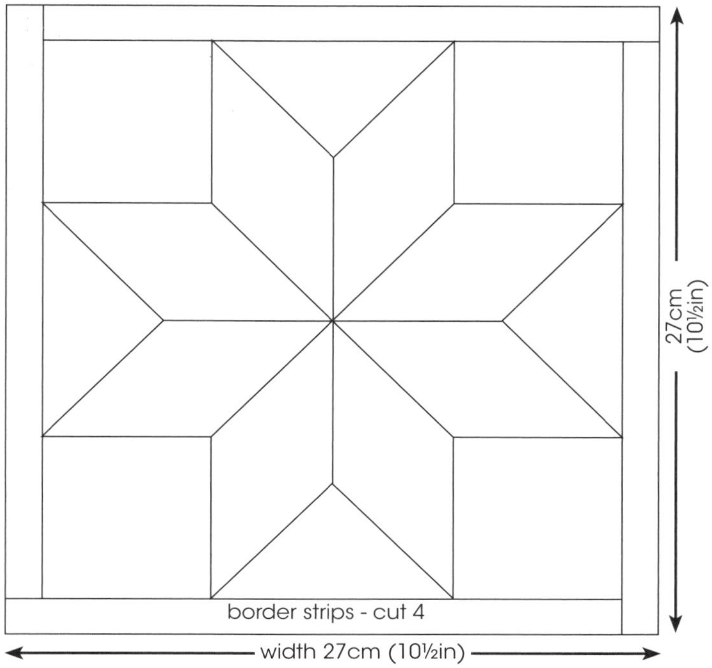

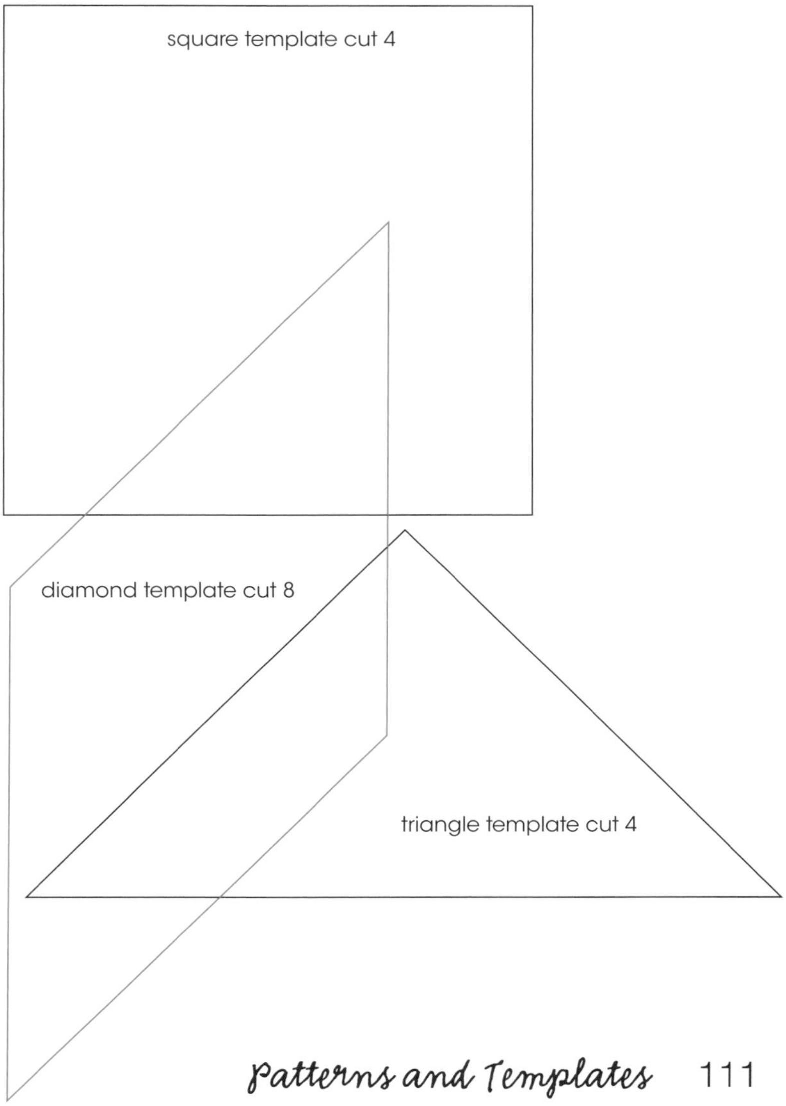

← width 10cm (8in) →

s/a

stitchline

fold

s/a

s/a

fold fold

stitchline

fold fold

stitchline

fold

stitchline

fold fold

stitchline

fold fold

stitchline

fold fold

stitchline

2cm
(¾in)

stitchline

finished
pocket width
8cm(3⅛in)

1cm
(⅜in)

fold

stitchline

s/a

Pocket strip A – cut 4 from calico and cut 4 from linen

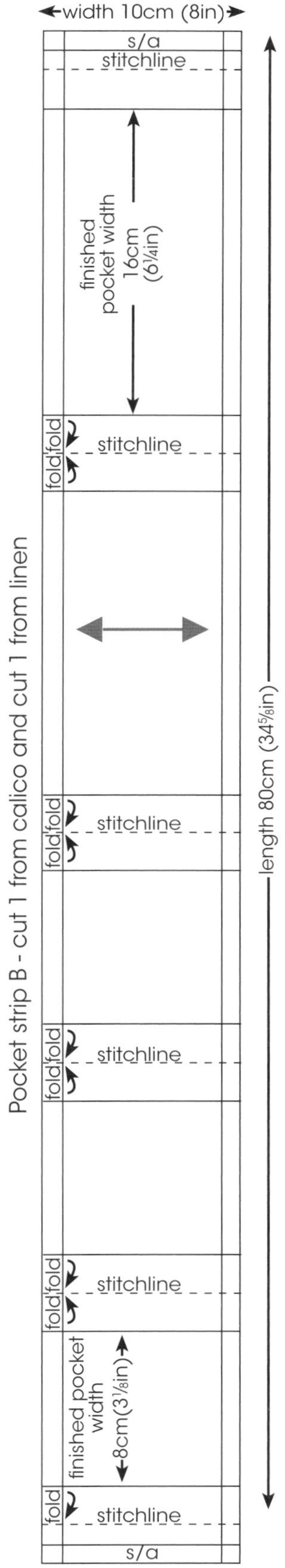

length 88cm (34⅝in)

← width 10cm (8in) →

s/a

stitchline

finished
pocket width
16cm
(6¼in)

fold fold

stitchline

fold fold

stitchline

fold fold

stitchline

fold fold

stitchline

fold
finished pocket
width
8cm(3⅛in)

fold

stitchline

s/a

Pocket strip B - cut 1 from calico and cut 1 from linen

length 80cm (34⅝in)

border strips - cut 4

27cm
(10½in)

width 27cm (10½in)

square template cut 4

diamond template cut 8

triangle template cut 4

Border strip template cut 4

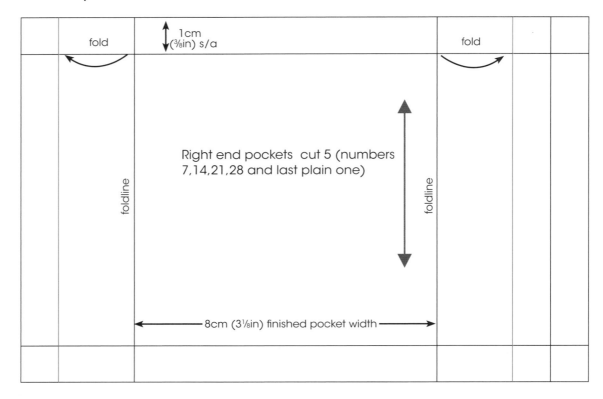

1cm (⅜in) s/a

fold

fold

foldline

foldline

Right end pockets cut 5 (numbers 7,14,21,28 and last plain one)

8cm (3⅛in) finished pocket width

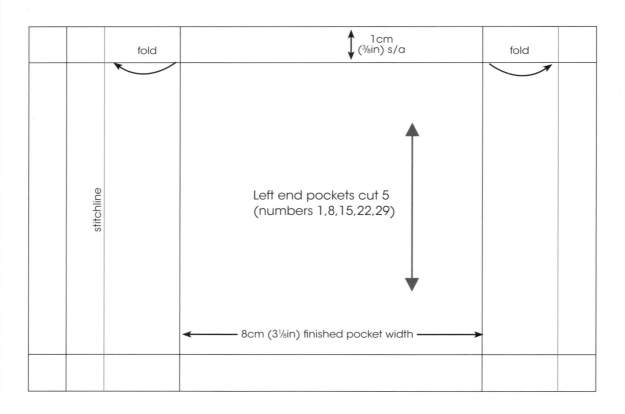

1cm (⅜in) s/a

fold

fold

stitchline

Left end pockets cut 5 (numbers 1,8,15,22,29)

8cm (3⅛in) finished pocket width

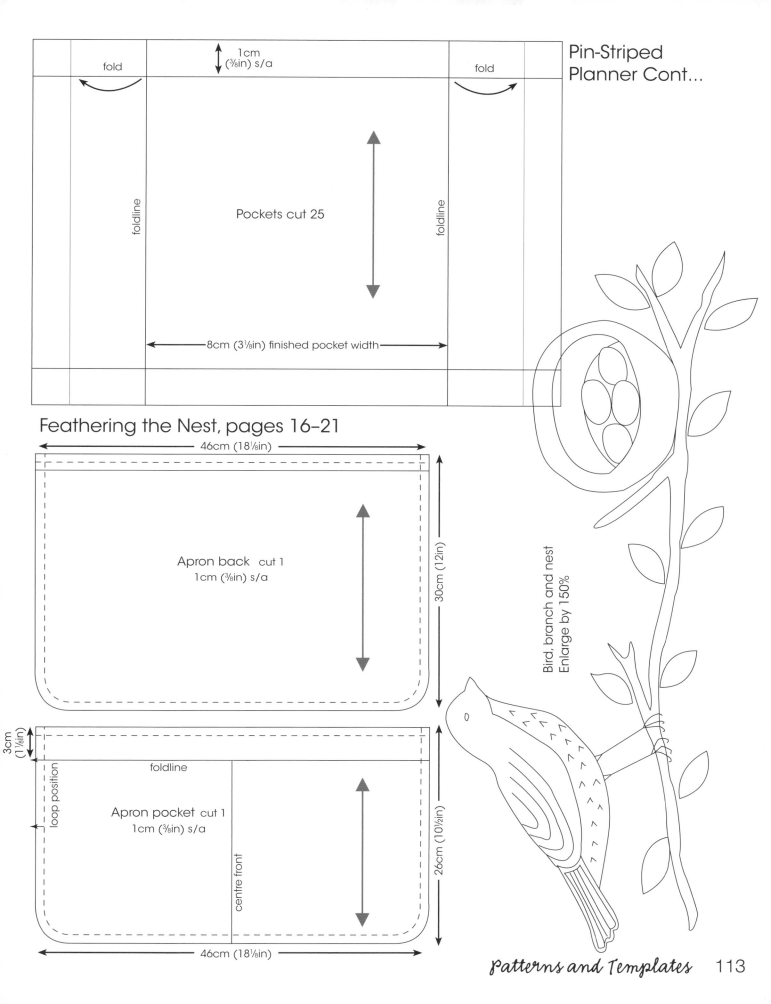

1cm
(⅜in) s/a

fold

foldline

Pockets cut 25

foldline

fold

←——— 8cm (3⅛in) finished pocket width ———→

## Feathering the Nest, pages 16–21

←——— 46cm (18⅛in) ———→

Apron back  cut 1
1cm (⅜in) s/a

30cm (12in)

Bird, branch and nest
Enlarge by 150%

3cm
(1⅛in)

loop position

foldline

Apron pocket  cut 1
1cm (⅜in) s/a

centre front

26cm (10½in)

←——— 46cm (18⅛in) ———→

*Patterns and Templates*  113

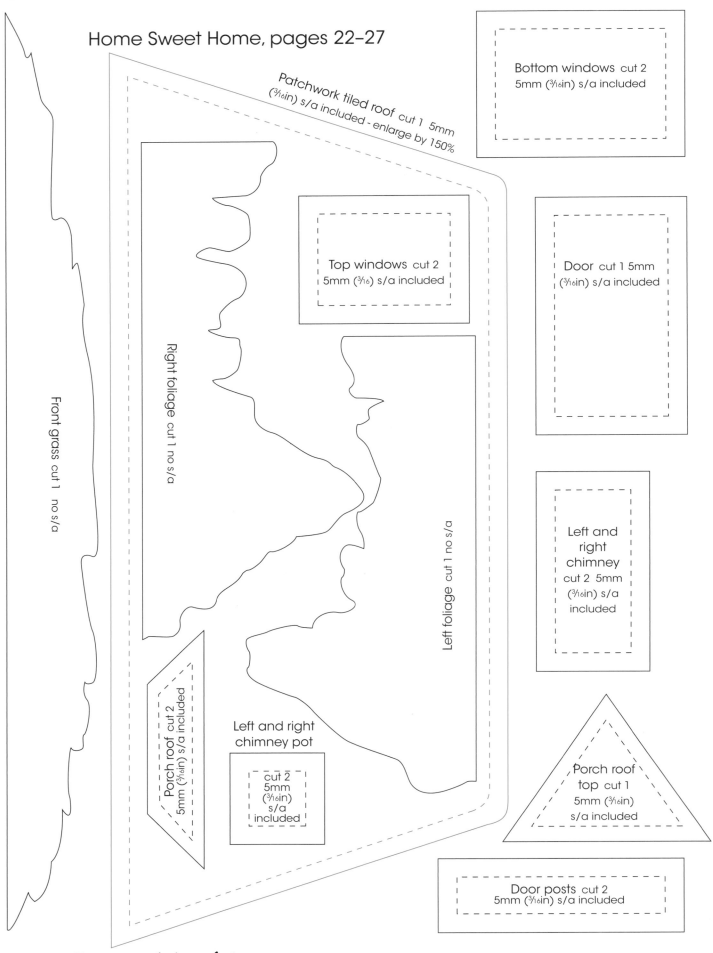

Home Sweet Home, pages 22–27

Patchwork tiled roof cut 1 5mm
(³⁄₁₆in) s/a included - enlarge by 150%

Front grass cut 1 no s/a

Right foliage cut 1 no s/a

Left foliage cut 1 no s/a

Top windows cut 2
5mm (³⁄₁₆) s/a included

Porch roof cut 2
5mm (³⁄₁₆in) s/a included

Left and right
chimney pot
cut 2
5mm
(³⁄₁₆in)
s/a
included

Bottom windows cut 2
5mm (³⁄₁₆in) s/a included

Door cut 1 5mm
(³⁄₁₆in) s/a included

Left and
right
chimney
cut 2 5mm
(³⁄₁₆in) s/a
included

Porch roof
top cut 1
5mm (³⁄₁₆in)
s/a included

Door posts cut 2
5mm (³⁄₁₆in) s/a included

114 *Patterns and Templates*

Strawberry stencils
cut 1 from acetate

Green stencil

Red stencil

Black outline
stencil

Appliqué Strawberry
actual size

# Sweet Dreams, pages 28-35
Flower appliqué

These templates are shown on the fold. Trace the shape then flip the tracing
 paper over on the foldline to complete the design.

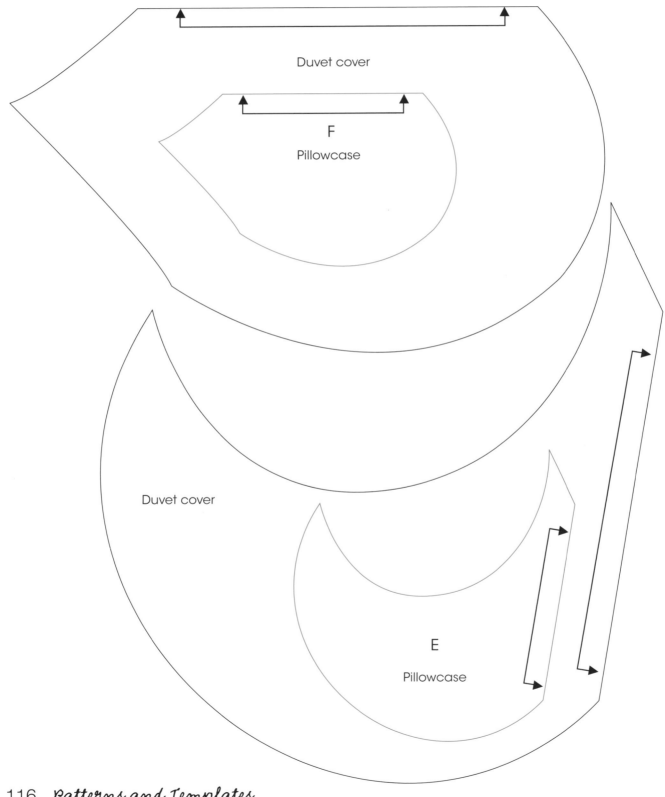

Duvet cover

F
Pillowcase

Duvet cover

E
Pillowcase

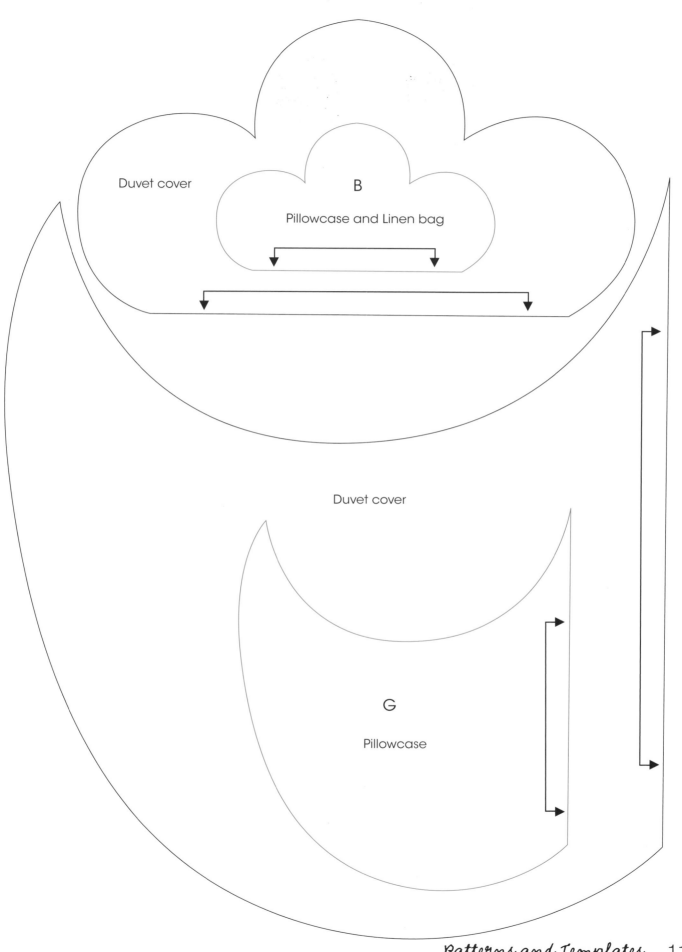

Duvet cover

B

Pillowcase and Linen bag

Duvet cover

G

Pillowcase

# Sweet Dreams cont...

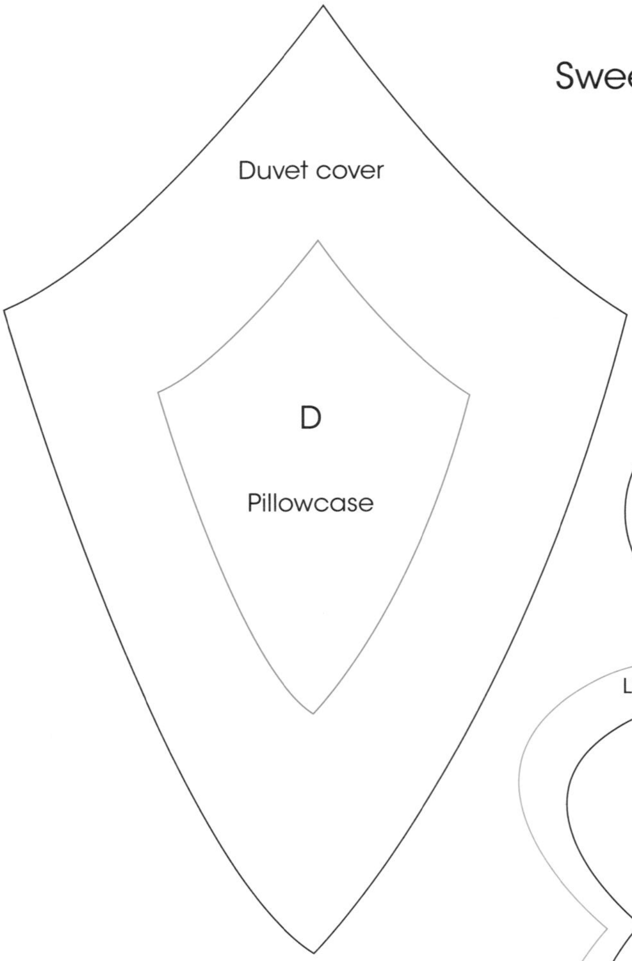

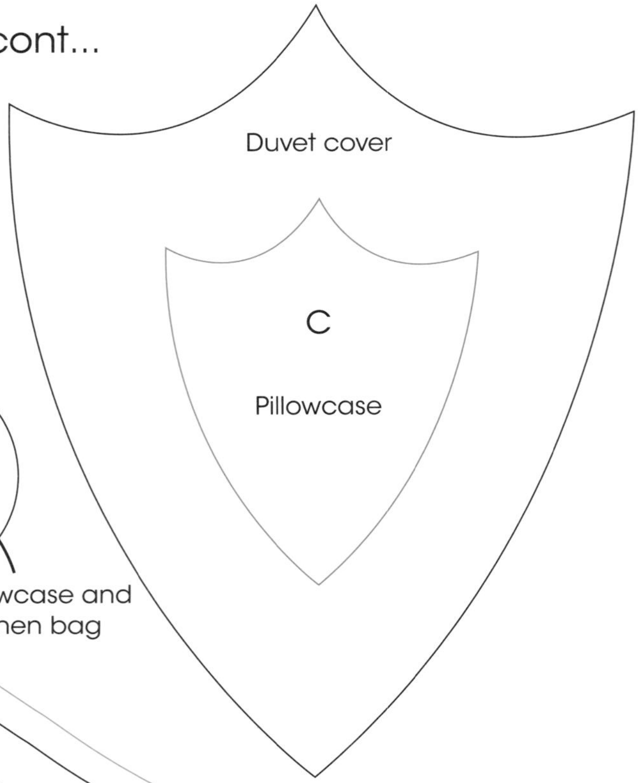

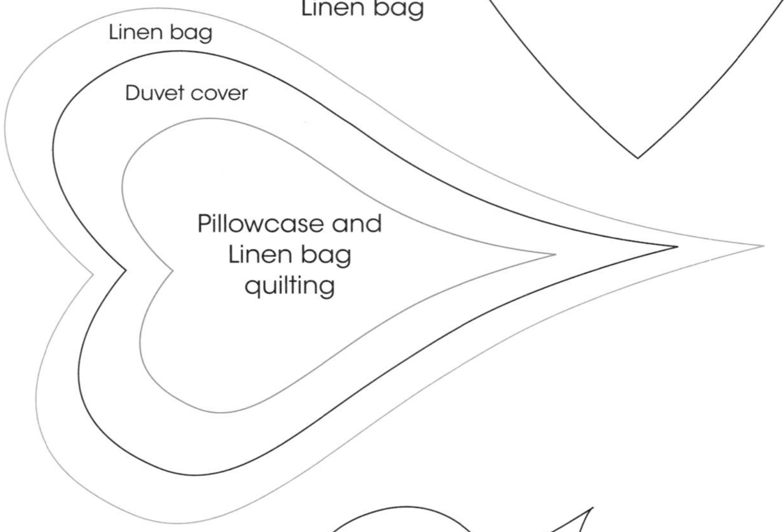

Duvet cover

D

Pillowcase

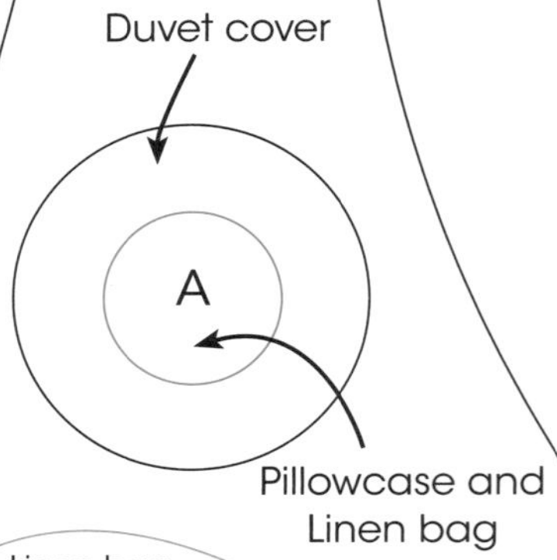

Duvet cover

A

Pillowcase and
Linen bag

C

Pillowcase

Duvet cover

Linen bag

Duvet cover

Pillowcase and
Linen bag
quilting

Tree of Life, pages 70–77

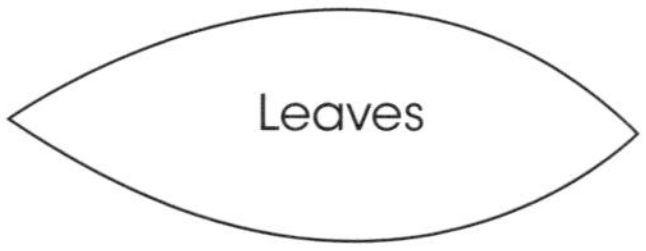

Leaves

Small apples

Apples

# Tree of Life cont...

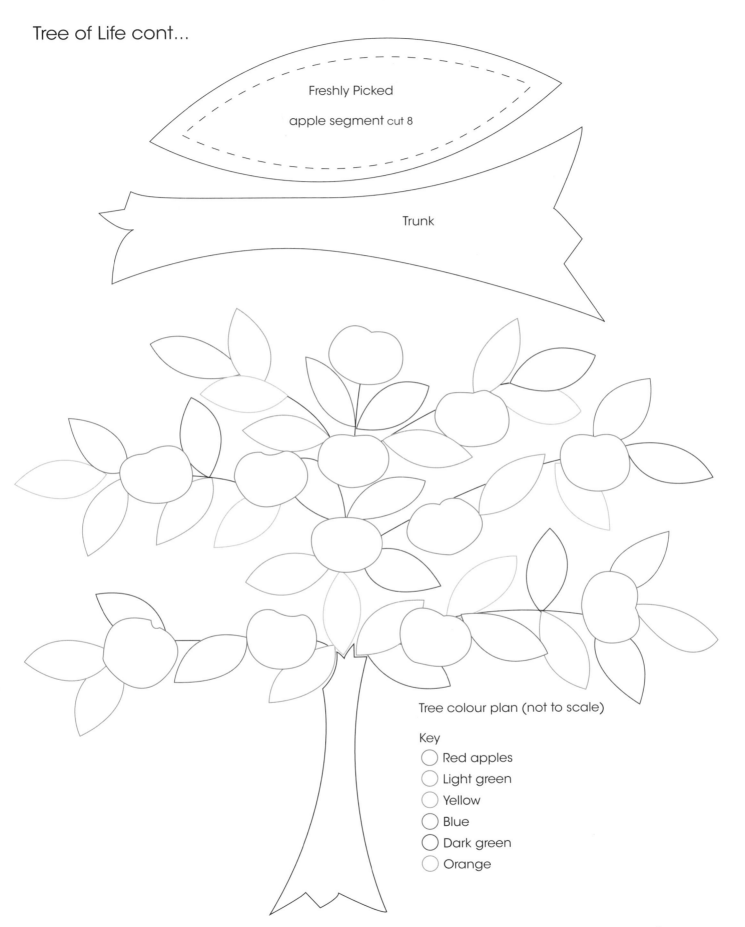

Freshly Picked

apple segment cut 8

Trunk

Tree colour plan (not to scale)

Key
- ○ Red apples
- ○ Light green
- ○ Yellow
- ○ Blue
- ○ Dark green
- ○ Orange

# Vintage Flowers, pages 36–43

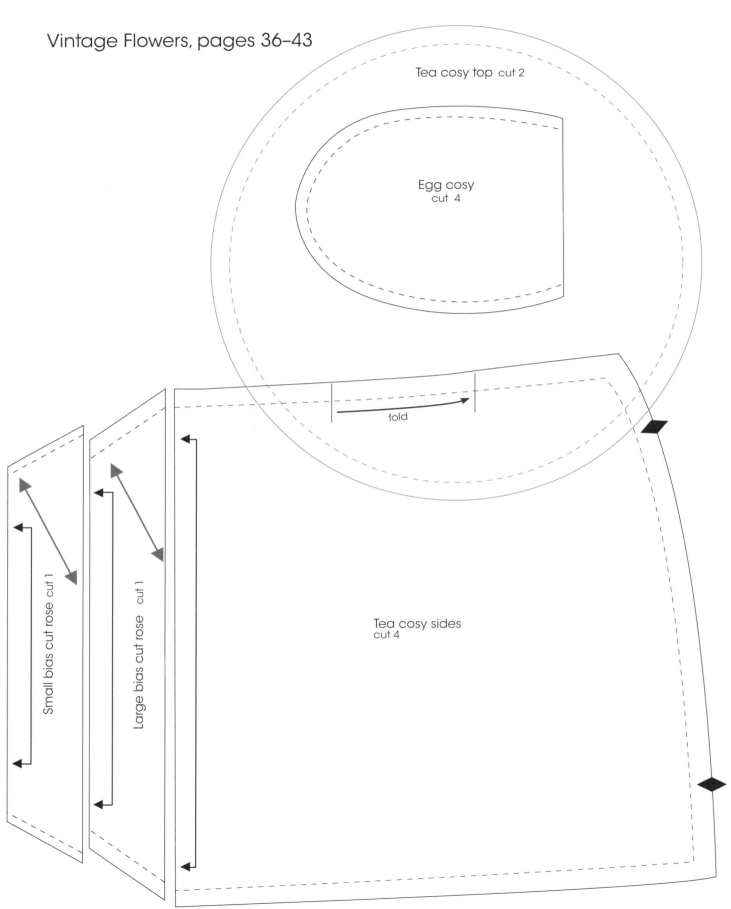

Tea cosy top cut 2

Egg cosy
cut 4

fold

Small bias cut rose cut 1

Large bias cut rose cut 1

Tea cosy sides
cut 4

# Vintage Flowers cont...

Embroidery patterns

(a)

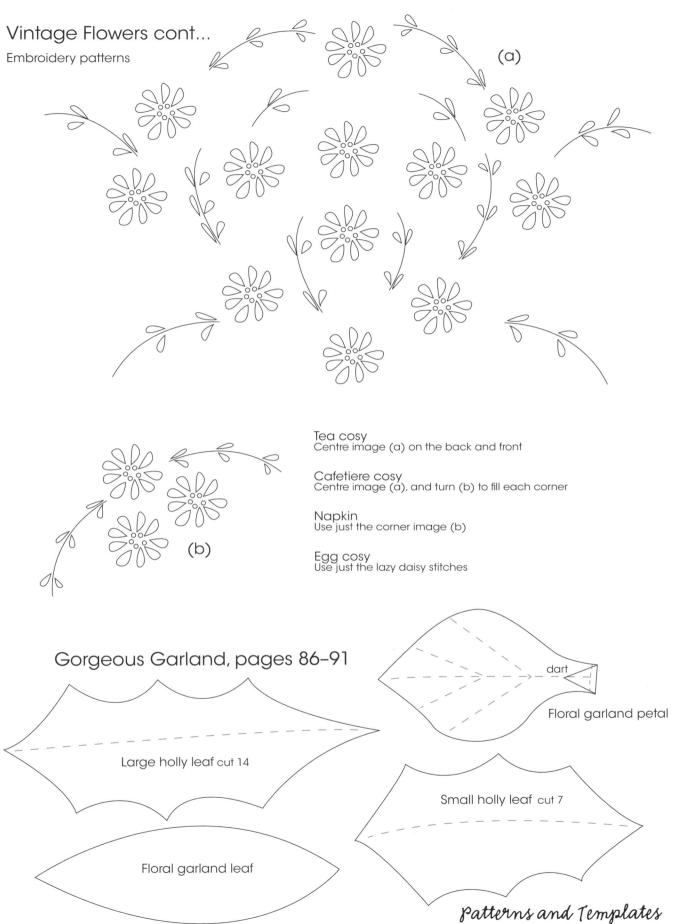

(b)

**Tea cosy**
Centre image (a) on the back and front

**Cafetiere cosy**
Centre image (a), and turn (b) to fill each corner

**Napkin**
Use just the corner image (b)

**Egg cosy**
Use just the lazy daisy stitches

# Gorgeous Garland, pages 86–91

dart

Floral garland petal

Large holly leaf cut 14

Small holly leaf cut 7

Floral garland leaf

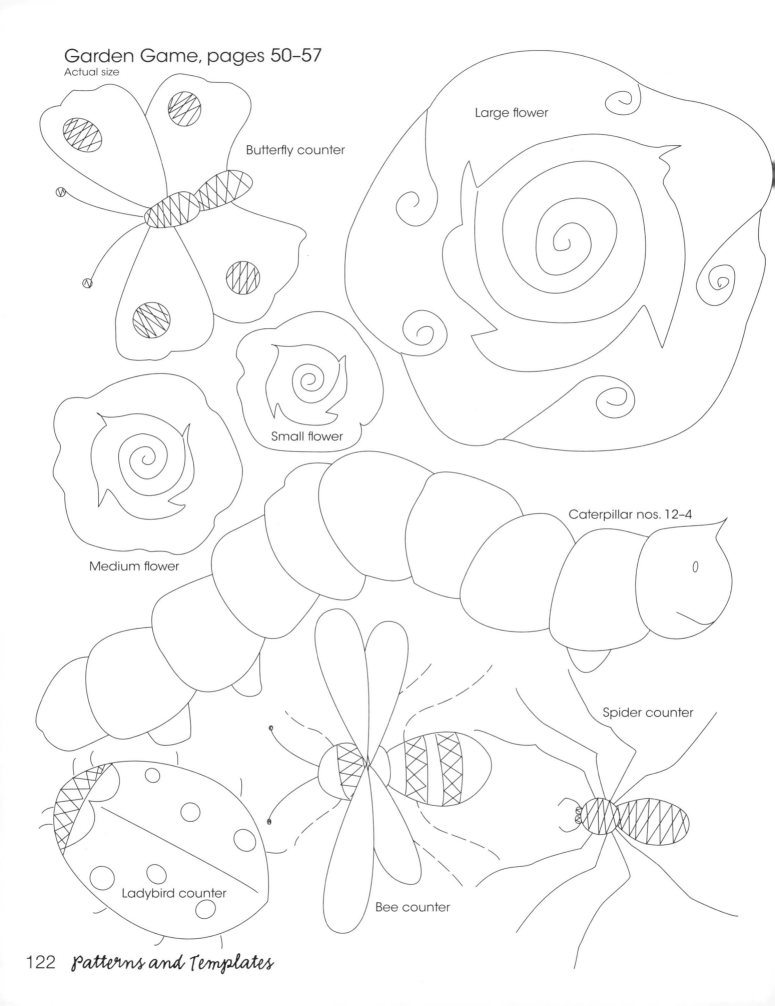

# Garden Game, pages 50–57

Actual size

Butterfly counter

Large flower

Small flower

Medium flower

Caterpillar nos. 12–4

Spider counter

Ladybird counter

Bee counter

# Garden Game cont...

Enlarge by 150 %

Reverse templates for Bondaweb

Flower stem nos. 56–39; nos. 48–3; nos. 24-7
Reverse this stem for nos. 52–21; 31–16; 27–5
Extend the stems freehand to reach the numbers indicated

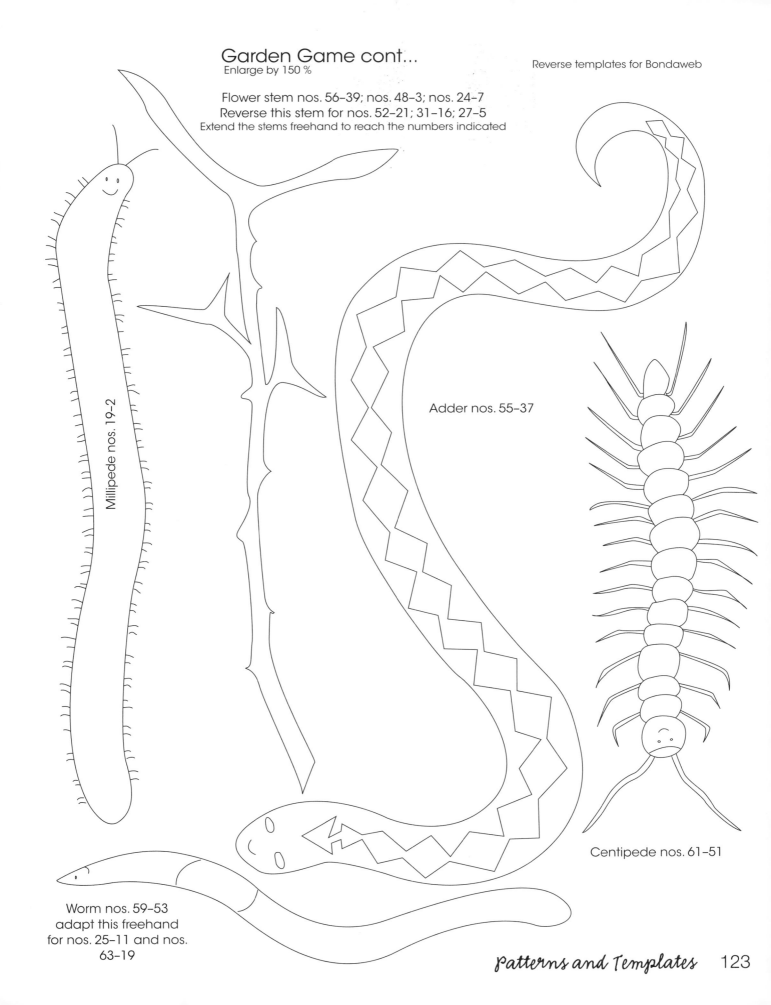

Millipede nos. 19-2

Adder nos. 55–37

Centipede nos. 61–51

Worm nos. 59–53
adapt this freehand
for nos. 25–11 and nos.
63–19

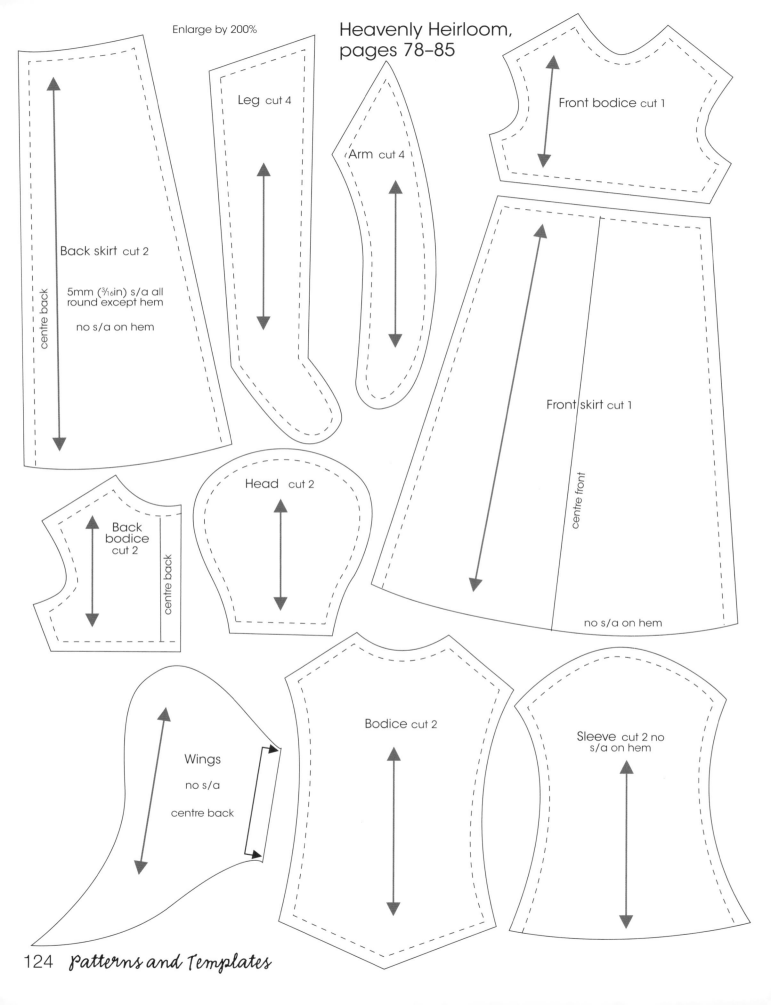

Enlarge by 200%

Heavenly Heirloom,
pages 78–85

Leg cut 4

Arm cut 4

Front bodice cut 1

Back skirt cut 2

5mm (3⁄16in) s/a all
round except hem

no s/a on hem

centre back

Front skirt cut 1

centre front

Back
bodice
cut 2

centre back

Head cut 2

no s/a on hem

Wings

no s/a

centre back

Bodice cut 2

Sleeve cut 2 no
s/a on hem

# Filled with Memories, pages 92–99

Front cover pattern and templates
Enlarge by 150%

0123456789

27cm
(10½in)

27cm
(10½in)

# suppliers

## UK Suppliers

**John Lewis**
Draycott Avenue
London, SW3 2NA
www.johnlewis.com
Retail craft, dress and furnishing
fabrics and haberdashery.

**The Eternal Maker**
89 Oving Road,
Chichester
West Sussex, PO19 7EW
www.eternalmaker.com
Wool felt, haberdashery, craft fabric
and lots more.

**Fabrics Galore**
52-54 Lavender Hill
Battersea
London, SW11 5RH
www.fabricsgalore.co.uk
End of line retail fabrics, including
designer names.

**Loop Fabrics**
32 West Hill Road
Brighton, BN1 3RT
www.loopfabric.co.uk
Retail and wholesale organic
and sustainable fabrics, including
cotton and hemp.

**Whaleys**
Harris Court,
Great Horton,
Bradford, BD7 4EQ
www.whaleys-bradford.ltd.uk
Wholesale and retail fabrics,
waddings and interfacing.

**Greenfibres**
99 High Street
Totnes
Devon, TQ9 5PF
www.greenfibres.co.uk
Organic and sustainable fabrics.

**Fibrecrafts**
Old Portsmouth Road
Peasmarsh
Guildford
Surrey, GU3 1LZ
www.fibrecrafts.com
Freezer paper, fabric paint,
rug canvas.

**Cheapfabrics.co.uk**
Thames Court
1 Victoria Street
Windsor
Berkshire, SL4 1YB
www.cheapfabrics.co.uk
Retail fabrics.

**MacCulloch and Wallis**
25–26 Dering Street
London
W1S 1AT
www.macculloch-wallis.co.uk
Millinery wire, fabrics and
haberdashery.

**Beadworks**
16 Redbridge Enterprise Centre
Thompson Close, Illford
Essex, IG1 1TY
www.beadworks.co.uk
Beads and jewellery wire.

## US Suppliers

**Beadbox**
1290 N. Scottsdale Road
Tempe Arizona 85281-1703
www.beadbox.com

**Distinctive Fabric**
2023 Bay Street
Los Angeles
CA 90021
www.distinctivefabric.com

**Gütermann of America Inc**
8227 Arrowbridge Blvd
POBox 7387
Charlotte
NC 28241-7387
Email:info@guttermann-us.com

**J&O Fabrics**
9401 Rt.130
Pennsauken
NJ 08110
www.jandofabrics.com

**Purl Patchwork**
147 Sullivan Street
New York
NY10012
www.purlsolo.com

**Reprodepot Fabrics**
www.reprodepot.com